Pustak Bharati

Issues of the Overseas Indians : Various Aspects

Prof. Ratnakar Narale
Dr. Rakesh Kumar Dubey

Pustak Bharati
Toronto, Canada

Pustak Bharati

Editors :
Dr. Ratnakar Narale, Ph.D (IIT), Ph.D. (Kalidas Sanskrit Univ.)
  Prof. Hindi. Ryerson University, Toronto.

Dr. Rakesh Kumar Dubey, Ph.D (Net), BHU, Varanasi.

Title :
Issues of the Overseas Indians : Various Aspects

Selected English articles of the Internationally well known authors, dealing with the life, issues, contribution and success of the Overseas Indians, with special emphasis on recognition of their efforts in preserving, propagating and promoting Bharatiya Sanskriti across the world.

Published by :
Pustak Bharati (Books-India), Toronto, Canada
www.pustak-bharati-canada.com
Pustak.bharati.canada@gmail.com

ISBN : 978-1-897416-28-0

Copywrite 2020

© All rights reserved. No part of this book may be copied, reproduced or utilised in any manner or by any means, computerised, e-mail, scanning, photocopying or by recording in any information storage and retrieval system, without the permission in writing from the Publisher.

Pustak Bharati

INDEX

Editorial

1. Sacrifice and Hardship of Indenrure Laboureres in Mauritius   1
   Allgoo Rajpalsingh, Mauritius

2. Two Diasporas: Overseas Chinese and Non-resident Indians   9
   In Their Homelands' Political Economy
   Dr. Veena Soni, Jodhpur, India

3. Indian Overseas Organization from Canada,   26
   Promoting Hindi, Sanskrit and Indian Culture in the world.
   Sunita Narale, Toronto, Canada

4. From India to Jamaica, Success story of a Pravasi   42
   Dr. Ratnakar Narale, Toronto, Canada

5. Overseas Literature of Indian Diaspora   60
   Dr. P.K. Pandia, Churu, Rajasthan

6. North-East India and the World : Mahabharata to the advent of Ahoms   65
   Narayan Singh Rao, Bikaner, India

7. India's Greatest Pravasi Mahatma   89
   Rupanuga Das, Thornhill, Canada

8. The emergence & expansion of the problems of the people of Indian Origin   98
   Rinkal Sharma, Delhi, India

Pustak Bharati

Editorial

Before the publication of the second issue of 'Pustak Bharati Patrika,' the international research journal of the Pustak Bharati, Toronto, Canada, a decision was made on 22 June 2019 to commemorate 100 years of complete termination of 'Bonded Slavery.' It was decided that the fourth issue of the Patrika will be 'Pravasi Special Issue' and it was also decided that an edited book on the same subject with Hindi and English Editions will also be published and made available worldwide through amazon.com. The Hindi Edition of this work is being Edited by our able Sub-Editor Dr. Rakesh Kumar Dubey of Varanasi, India.

With the efforts of Mahamana Pt. Madan Mohan Malaviya ji, the 'Bonded Labor slavery,' was declared a stigma on Indian civilization, and end to it in the year 1915-16. At this time, the Second World War was going on and by this time the laborers who had written a 5-year indenture could not be liberated immediately. Their complete emancipation of this evil was achieved only in 1920-21 and with this, this utterly inhuman practice came to an end.

The year 2020-21 is the 100th year of complete abolition of the indentured system, known in history as the most cruel system. This year is definitely the most memorable to the present children of Indian laborers who were taken to the colonies as indentured laborers as well as those in India. It is especially memorable for the people of the country, because due to this practice, the innocent and civilized people of India were taken to the colonies and there they were treated worst than animals by the so-called civilized European Nations. Due to this practice, the culture of India, which taught the world lesson of civilization, was severely degraded and it came to be known as the 'country of coolies' in the world. The vested economic interest with which the European Countries established this practice, it will remain inscribed on his forehead as 'a stigma' for the centuries to come.

Slavery is not a new system. Evidence of its practice is found in one form or another in the history of most countries of the world. Just as the geographical exploration and spread of European Civilization started as a result of the Renaissance in Europe, along with it, for the sake of economic benefit, the countries of Europe also started the heinous act of slave trade, under which the Habsi People of the continent of Africa were taken by force in the Europe and America and treated as unconditional slaves.

But gradually the movement against this inhuman practice started in Europe and after the defeat of Napoleon, it was agreed to abolish the practice of slavery in the Vienna Congress (1814-1815) and after which this practice was ceased. Even in England this practice was declared illegal in 1833.

Editorial

After the end of this practice, the people of Europe living in the colonies started to get ruined and they requested the Company Government of India for help. Slavery was abolished in the world and its recurrence was impossible. Thus, the British started a new practice and named it 'Indentured System' 'Miyadi System,' or 'Girmitiya System'.

In this way, when the practice of slavery vanished from the world, the British in 1834 AD for the benefit of their own kind converted the same practice in India and named it 'Betabandi System' which was nothing but a slavery, in the minds of the Indian people.

The slave trade is disguised as a Cooli System.
Never seen such till now, in the Country of India.

Under this custom, the Indians were lured into the colonies of Africa, the Caribbean, South-East Asia and the former French colonies, where their lives were filled with tortures. After the end of this practice, the offspring of the descendants of the Indians in the colonies were not suddenly rejuvenated. They had to struggle for their rights for many decades. In addition new willful immigrants arrived in these countries outside India to make their homes as NRIs. These people of Indian origin worked together in the areas of education, politics, business, social uplift, cultural co-ordination and at the same time for the protection of their culture while not opposing the local people.

While living in the colonies and the Western Countries, the Girmitiya and the NRI Indian people grew there with their hard work and through continuous struggles. They made valuable contribution to the political, social, economic and cultural progress of these countries. While living in the Girmitia countries, the Indian people overseas who successfully connected themselves with the local people and their culture, while at the same time keeping their language, culture, traditions and heritage far away from India. Indian NRI people who went abroad after independence have also made priceless contribution in preserving and spreading Indian culture and are engaged doing it day and night. In this book, tries to throw little light on these aspects.

Toronto, Canada
Friday, March 27, 2020

Prof. Ratnakar Narale
Editor-in-Chief, Pustak Bharati,
Toronto, Canada.

Sacrifice and Hardship of Indenture Labourers in Mauritius

Allgoo Rajpalsingh, Mauritius

Introduction of Mauritius

According to history Mauritius was inhabitedit was discovered by the Arabs and Malays, the Portuguese seaman Domingo Fernandez Pereira sighted Mauritius in 1507 and Named It "Ilha Do Cerne" (Island of the Swan). The Group of islands, which is Mauritius, Rodrigues, and Reunion were named Mascarenes after the Portuguese Captain, Pero Mascarenhas and today this group of islands is still known as the Mascarene Islands. However, the Portuguese never settled in the country, they used the island as a port of call and a source of fresh foods as they were more interested in protecting their trade routes with India.

The Dutch Settlements

Wybrant Warwijck was the first Dutchman who visited the country in 1598 and renamed the island after the Dutch Stadtholder Maurits (known also as Maurice of Nassau - Prince of Orange). During the first years, the Dutch did not occupy the island but regularly visited it benefiting from its raw materials such as ebony and wild animals like the famous Dodo, pigs, goats and tortoises.

The first Dutch settlement started in 1630, mainly in order to prevent the French and the British to occupy the island. The Hollanders settled on the east coast of the island where the south-eastern harbor is, an area which they called "Haven van Warwijck", where the town of Vieux Grand Port now stands.

Allgoo Rajpalsingh, Mauritius

The Dutch East India Company sent Simons Gooyer to become the governor of the island together with a group of twenty five men, they established the first settlement. The aim of the settlement was to sent ebony trees and wood to Batavia and Holland, to find Ambergris (used for producing expensive perfumes), produce food and tobacco, rear cattle and fowls for settlers, supply fresh food and products for the Dutch ships travelling along the naval route, build a fort to protect the harbor and especially to prevent the French and English from using or occupying the island.

In 1638, the Dutch built a square wooden fort with bastions and cannons at each corner to protect the harbor, the fort was named Fort Frederik Hendrik. After the reign of Simons Gooyer, Governor Van Der Stel landed in the island, and brought with him various seeds and fruits including sugar cane saplings.

He also brought rabbits, sheep, geese, ducks, pigeons and stags, which multiplied over years and were sources of fresh provisions to passing ships. In order to cut down ebony trees for exportation, Van Der Stel needed more men power, so he went to Madagascar where he obtained 105 slaves.

During a period of three years Governor Van Der Stel full attention was given to agriculture: cultivated rice, indigo, tobacco and cane. Unfortunately the crops and fort were not long lasting and they were badly damaged by a cyclone in 1644.

Discouraged by the bad conditions in Mauritius of droughts, storms, rats and monkeys which prevented agricultural progress, the Dutch decided to abandon the island. Then at 1710 the Dutch tried to settle again in Mauritius but this time with some skilled man like carpenters, blacksmiths, tanners, sawyers, and brewers. But again due to the droughts, cyclones and pests problem, the new settlers abandoned the island.

Allgoo Rajpalsingh, Mauritius

The French Period
For some years following the Dutch departure, Mauritius remained unoccupied. In 1715, Captain Gillaume Dufresne D'Arsel occupied the island for France and gave it the name of Isle de France. Settlers arrived to the Island from Bourbon Island and from France. Denis Denyon was assigned as governor and settlements started in Port North West (Port-Louis) and Port South East (Grand Port). Acres of land were cleared and tobacco maize and rice were planted but again were soon destroyed by cyclones.

In 1734, Bertrand Mahé de Labourdonnais, a great sailor and trader was appointed governor of the island. He transferred the head quarters of the island from Port South East to Port North West. During his governorship he built roads, a big civil and military hospital which still exists near the harbor. He also built the Government house, Pamplemousses Garden, Chateau de mon Plaisir, Powder magazines, stores, ware houses, the harbor, canals and a line of fortifications and batteries to defend the capital. Bertrand Mahé de Labourdonnais encouraged settlers to cultivate their land and obtained slaves from Mozambique to help them. The settlers planted sugarcane, wheat, rice, cotton, coffee and indigo, and built the first factory at Pamplemousses.

To carry out public works and to cultivate more lands, Indian sailors and artisans were brought to the island. At that time many developments were made which changed Ile de France into a prosperous colony.

In 1767 the crown took over the island from East India Company, and Governor Dumas and Intendant Pierre Poivre were the new administrators. The latter was a great botanist and has brought pepper and cinnamon plants from Moluccas and other spices from Philippines. Under their rule roads were straighten and widened, and many stone houses were build in Port-Louis (few still exist today).

The British Captivating Mauritius
The British made several efforts to conquer Mauritius, but these efforts were deflected by the French. It was during the Napoleonic Wars that the British invaded Mauritius in 1810.

Allgoo Rajpalsingh, Mauritius

The British's main focus in captivating Mauritius was to protect their main sea route from England to British India from the French who threatened the British shipping and naval route.

On 1810, the British landed at Cap Malheureux with a greater number of forces and 174 strong guns against the 144 guns of the French. The battle continued without interruption until the French which were outnumbered had to surrender.

Once the British captivated the island, in order to gain the support of the locals the British guaranteed the inhabitants that their customs, lalanguage and culture will be respected.

Ile de France was renamed Mauritius and it was formally given to Britain at the Treaty of Paris in 1815. Sir Robert Farquar who became the first British governor of Mauritius made rapid social and economic changes. In August 1833 the law of abolishing slavery was passed by the British parliament and came into force in Mauritius in 1835. The abolition of slavery had important repercussions on the socio-economic and demographic fields. This resulted in turning to India, from where the local planters brought a large number of indentured laborers to work in the sugar cane fields.

Indentured labour from South Asia (1834-1917)

After the abolition of slavery, newly free men and women refused to work for the low wages on offer on the sugar farms in British colonies in the West Indies. Indentured labour was a system of bonded labour that was instituted following the abolition of slavery. Indentured labour were recruited to work on sugar, cotton and tea plantations, and rail construction projects in British colonies in West Indies, Africa and South East Asia. From 1834 to the end of the WWI, Britain had transported about 2 million Indian indentured workers to 19 colonies including Fiji, Ceylon, Trinidad, Guyana, Malaysia, Uganda, Kenya and South Africa including Mauritius...

The indentured workers (known derogatively as "coolies") those were recruited from India, and signed a contract in their own countries to work abroad for a period of 5 years or more. They were meant to receive wages, a small amount of land and in some cases, promise of a return passage once their contract was over. In reality, this seldom happened, and the conditions were harsh and their wages

The indentured workers sought to escape poverty and famines that were a frequent occurrence during the period of British colonial rule in India. But given the high levels of illiteracy, few workers understood the terms of the contract they put their thumb imprint to (in lieu of a signature, as they could not write). Many were commonly misled about where they were departing for and the wages they would receive. Through testimonies of the migrants we now know that many workers were recruited from rural India to work in cities like U.P. Bihar, Tamil Naidu, , but once there were tricked or persuaded to sign the contract which took them to the emigration depot and to the plantations overseas.

The journey took between 10 and 20 weeks, depending on the destination. **Conditions on the ships** were similar to those on slave ships. In 1856-57, the average death rate for Indians travelling to the Caribbean was 17% due to diseases like dysentery, cholera and measles. After they disembarked, there were further deaths in the holding depot and during the process of acclimatisation in the colonies (Tinker, 1993).

Allgoo Rajpalsingh, Mauritius

They were under a five-year contract and had to work either in the sugarcane fields or the factories. Each month, one rupee was deduced from their salary to pay for their return trip to India, They earned Rs.5/month, two pounds of rice, half a pound of 'dhal', two ounces of coconut oil, two ounces of mustard oil and salted fish. At the end of year, their employer would provide them with a shirt, two sheets, a jacket, a cap, a 'dhoti' – or a total of eight yards of 'kaliko' - and two covers. The ration for the women and children was to a lesser extent.

The funds saved through the Rs.1/month deduction were restituted to them if they chose to stay in Mauritius. The trip to Calcutta cost £3.45 shillings, to Madras £2.19 shillings and to Bombay (Mumbai) £3.18 shillings.

Working Conditions in the plantations

The conditions at work were harsh, with long **working hours** and low wages. Given the weak physical condition of the labourers after the long voyage, this took its toll.. Children were expected to work alongside their parents from the time they were 7 years old.

The ex-indentured worker told: "We were whipped for small mistakes. If you woke up late, i.e. later than 4 am, during the crop season you got whipped. No matter what happened, whether there was rain or thunder you had to work 4.30 am - we were there to work and work we had to done, otherwise we were abused and beaten up between 1895 and 1902, several thousand Indian indentured labourers helped also to build Road construction projects

On the constitutional plane, the Council of Government which was first established in 1825, was enlarged in 1886 to make room for elected representatives. The new Council of Government included 10 members elected on a restricted franchise.

It was not until 1933 that the Constitution was significantly amended. But the Constitution was still restricted to persons within a certain income bracket and to property owners. A major breakthrough occurred in 1948, when after years of protracted negotiations for a more liberal Constitution, franchise was extended to all adults who could pass a simple literacy test. The Council of Government was replaced by a Legislative Council composed of 19 elected members, 12 members nominated by the Governor and three ex-officio members. General elections were held in August 1948 and the first Legislative Council met on 1st
September 1948.

Allgoo Rajpalsingh, Mauritius

Mauritius Independence

Following Constitutional conferences held in London in 1955 and 1957, the ministerial system was introduced and general elections were held on 9th March 1959.

In 1961, a Constitutional Review Conference was held in London and a programme of further Constitutional advance was established. It was followed in 1965 by the last Constitutional Conference which paved the way for Mauritius to achieve independence.

Resistance to the indenture system

Migrant workers did try to oppose the abuses of the indentured labour system, but this was difficult. Some sent petitions to the agents of the colonial government who administered the indenture system. According to historical records, indentured workers carried out acts of sabotage and revenge against the plantation owners on numerous occasions, but this just resulted in increased repression.

To the voices of the indentured workers was added the dissenting voice of the growing Indian nationalist movement. Mahatma Gandhi, the leader of the Indian freedom movement, saw first-hand the plight of Asian indentured labourers in South Africa and campaigned on this issue during the first decade of the 20th century. The system of indentured labour was officially abolished by British government in 1917.

Today, through the Aapravasi Ghat, where landed the Indian immigrants, their descendants pay homage to the memory of those hard workers, every 2nd of November. Thanks to Mr Bikhramsing Ramlallah, a former member of Legislative Assembly and Journalist, this date has been a landmark in the remembrance of indentured labourers' legacy in Mauritius. But now the time is ripe to also remember all those who fought for the rights of the Indian immigrants.

Thanks to the fighters like de Plevitz, Curé, Anquetil, Ramnarain, Jugdambi and others. Workers' struggles of the 30s and 40s often come to my mind. Those were difficult days indeed. But thanks to the efforts of those pioneers, a wind of change had started blowing over the workers' world.

It is with fond nostalgia that I recall some of the early fighters and the periods of unrest often punctuated with strikes:
As a militant for the cause of the workers of this country, I have dedicated my whole career to the fight for their rights. I have been at the forefront of several important workers' actions and forced acceptable solutions to knotty industrial disputes.

Allgoo Rajpalsingh, Mauritius

Free General Elections in Mauritius

The first free general elections were held in Mauritius on 7 August 1948- under a new constitution which established a Legislative Council with 19 elected members, 12 appointed members and 3 Ex officio members and expanded the franchise to all adults who could write their name in one of the islands languages. They were won by the labour Party led by Guy Rozemont with eleven of the 19 elected seats.in 1953 general elections was also won by Labour Party. The General Elections of Prior 19 Gov67 was held under a new constitution The Government was formed by the party or group which control a majority on the unicameral legislature. The National Assembly has 70 members, 62 elected for a five year tearm in 21 multi-member constituency and 8 additional "best loser" memebrs appointed by the Supreme Court.

References:

L'Express ; Le Mauricien; National Library; Aapravasi Library;
Le Mouvement Syndicale a Ile Maurice;
A Brief History of Trade Unionism In Mauritius

Two Diasporas: Overseas Chinese and Non-resident Indians In Their Homelands' Political Economy

Dr. Veena Soni[1]

ABSTRACT

This paper, through a comparative study of the roles Chinese and Indian diasporas in the United States play in the political economy of their respective homelands, explores the relationship between the diaspora and homeland development and how this dynamic relationship contributes to economic growth and foreign relations of the homelands. The author argues that the roles of Indian and Chinese diasporas in their respective homelands' development consistently reflect, and are heavily influenced by, their homelands' economic development strategies as well as political history and culture. The author also argues that the impact of the diaspora on the foreign relations of their homelands is conditional upon the state of bilateral relations between their homeland and the country of residence. This study raises issues for future research, such as the relationship between the diasporas and regime type of the homeland. The author concludes by suggesting that since activities of overseas Chinese and non-resident Indians provide a unique perspective in the comparative study of Chinese and Indian political economy, the two diasporas warrant more scholarly and policy attention.

Keywords: *diaspora, overseas Chinese, non-resident Indians, international political economy, US policies towards China and India*

INTRODUCTION

India and China are two emerging Asian powers that have many commonalities such as a huge population, a long history, rich cultural traditions, Western colonial legacy, and a large diaspora community around the world. Yet the two countries took a different path in terms of political and economic developments after they gained national independence in the late 1940s. People who are interested in India and China often compare the two nations and ask why they are very different in many respects today.

---

[1] DR.VEENA SONI (POST-DOCTORAL FELLOW), JAI NARAYAN VYAS UNIVERSITY, JODHPUR (RAJ)

Some have sought answers in history, culture, political institutions, economic systems, government polices, leadership, etc. Though much progress has been made in the comparative study of the political economy of India and China, one area that has attracted scant attention is the role of the diaspora in each country's economic development and foreign relations.

India and China both have a large diaspora population. The Indian diaspora is currently estimated to number approximately 20 million, and there are estimated 55 million Chinese in over 135 countries.[1] Though traditionally the majority of Chinese diaspora have lived in Southeast Asia and the majority of Indian diaspora in Southeast Asia, the Middle East and Africa, in recent decades tens of thousands of Chinese and Indians have immigrated to North America and other developed regions. And many of these new Asian immigrants to the West tend to be young, highly educated, and often wealthy. According to the 2000 US Census, Chinese Americans, numbered about 2.7 million, is the largest Asian group in the United States. Asian Indians from the subcontinent, though fewer in number, with 1.9 million, are generally better educated and enjoy higher personal incomes than both Chinese Americans and Japanese Americans.[2] The lives and activities of these Asian diasporas and their unique position in bridging the East and the West and in promoting their homelands' development and foreign relations are not well known to many.

This paper, through a comparative study of similarities and differences of the roles played by Chinese and Indian diasporas in the political economy of their respective ancestral homelands, explores the relations between the diaspora and homeland development and how this dynamic relationship contributes to economic growth and foreign relations of the homelands. I contend that the roles of Indian and Chinese diasporas in the development of their homelands consistently reflect, and are heavily influenced by, the economic development strategies as well as political history and culture of their home countries. Comparing activities of the two diasporas in the United States, I argue that their impact on the foreign relations of their homelands is conditional on the state of bilateral relations between their homelands and the United States. The contributions of diasporas are likely to become more prominent in China's and India's political economy in the 21st century as the two nations continue to woo their expatriates. This often neglected aspect of contemporary political economy warrants further scholarly and policy attention by the international community. The study of diasporas and their roles in both their countries of residence and countries of origin also provides a unique vantage point from which to study international political economy in general.

HYPOTHESES

Literature on diaspora and international migration in general abounds in such fields as history, sociology, anthropology, and geography. Relatively speaking, the paucity of literature on the role of diaspora in the economic development and foreign relations of their homelands is unmistakably obvious in the field of political science and international relations. A number of political scientists have studied various aspects of diasporic movements. Among others, Cohen (1997), Sheffer (2003), King and Melvin (1998), Wang (1991, 2000), and Shain (1994) have researched characteristics of selected diaspora groups such as the Jews, the Russians, the Chinese, and ethnic diasporas' role in US foreign policy, but very few study has been done to systematically compare the Chinese and Indian diasporas.

Traditionally the study of diaspora is often placed in the larger context of international migration. In the international migration literature, four major schools of thought have attempted to account for the causal processes of international migration: neoclassical theories that focus on factors causing economic disruption and migration; market theories that emphasize the failure of the markets in the sending nations as the barrier to economic advancement; relative deprivation theory that assumes that migrants have a strong desire to improve their income so as to "keep up with the Joneses" in their communities; and the segmented labor market theory that sees global migration as demand driven in advanced industrial societies where economy divides employment into a primary sector and a secondary sector.[3] However, little research has been conducted to explain whether and how diaspora activities and homeland political economy are interrelated.

An interesting phenomenon in the extant literature on Chinese and Indian diasporas is a handful of articles about how India should learn from China in attracting diasporic investment.[4] A vigorous comparative study of why and how the two countries differ in this respect is lacking. How overseas Chinese and non-resident Indians help promote relations between their homeland and their host country also remains understudied. For example, what government policies and practices in China and India might have contributed to the differences? What are the institutions and their roles in attracting diaspora groups and their resources? Why has China done a better job so far in attracting diasporic investment? How do the activities of Asian diaspora communities in the United States affect US foreign policy towards Asia? This research attempts to address some of these important questions. To compare and contrast the two diasporas, this paper proposes the following hypotheses:

H1: The role of the diaspora in the development of its homeland consistently reflects, and is heavily influenced by, the economic development strategies as well as political history and culture of the homeland.

H2: The impact of the diaspora on the foreign relations of its homeland is conditional on the state of bilateral relations between the homeland and country of residence.

To test the hypotheses, I first collect data and cases on how Indian and Chinese diasporas have contributed to the economic development and foreign relations of their home countries respectively. For their contributions to the homeland's economic development, I focus on their investment; for their roles in homeland's foreign relations, I focus on their activities in the United States and explore how they influence US policies towards China and India.

Then we compare empirical findings to study the differences and similarities in the behaviors of the two diasporas. Explanations will be developed to account for similar and different activities of Chinese and Indian diasporas from historical, cultural, economic, institutional, and geopolitical perspectives. The article concludes with a brief discussion of the significance of this research in the study of international political economy.

EMPIRICAL FINDINGS I: DIASPORAS AND HOMELANDS' ECONOMIC DEVELOPMENT

China and India are enjoying some of the fastest rising economic growth rates in the world. But their political regimes and basic economic strategies have been different, and both have come a long way after their national independence in the late 1940s. Table 1 summarizes the basic characteristics of Chinese and Indian economies. An obvious major difference is the foreign direct investment each country has received since 1990.

Table 1 Competing Giants: a Tale of Two Economies[5]

	China	India
Per capita GDP (PPP, 2006 est.)	$7,700	$3,800
Economic reform start year	1979	1991
Average annual GDP growth rate (1990-2000)	9.6 percent	5.5 percent
GDP growth rate (2006)	10.7 percent	9.2 percent
Economic strength	Manufacturing	Services
FDI in 1990	3.5 billion	0.4 billion

FDI in 2004	61 billion	5.5 billion
Diaspora's contribution to FDI average	60-70%*	< 10%

SOURCES: 1. *The World Factbook*, CIA, June 2007.
2. The US-China Business Council, "Foreign Investment in China, 2004," accessed online from http://www.uschina.org on May 3, 2006.
3. Reserve Bank of India Annual Report, 2004-05.
4. *World Investment Report 2003* by UN Conference on Trade and Development.
5. Huang, Yasheng, and Tarun Khanna, "Can India Overtake China?" *Foreign Policy* (July/August 2003), pp. 74-81.

After failed socialism, self-isolation and a serious financial crisis, India officially started economic reform in 1991, a dozen years later than China. Whereas overseas Chinese have contributed as much as 70% of China's total foreign direct investment over the past 15 years, the Indian diaspora has provided less than 10% for India.[6]

As will be explained later, in addition to the fact that India's market economic reform started much later than China's, a series of other factors also contribute to the vast differences in the relationship between Indian and Chinese diasporas and their home country's development respectively.[7]

EMPIRICAL FINDINGS II: DIASPORAS AND HOMELANDS' RELATIONS WITH THE UNITED STATES

Overseas Chinese and non-resident Indians are two relatively successful ethnic groups in many parts of the world. These diasporas have succeeded in such fields as business, sciences, engineering, the arts, medicine, education, restaurant and other service industries, etc. Because of their diligence and success, and the rich cultures of their countries of origin, overseas Chinese and non-resident Indians are generally well respected in Western societies. The fascinating ancient cultures, growing markets, exotic foods and customs may all have helped the two groups in bridging their countries of residence and their countries of origin. Most of these diasporas maintain close emotional, cultural, economic and even political links to their homelands.

Chinese and Indian diaspora communities in the United States are staunch supporters of close Chinese-American and Indian-American relations respectively. In foreign policy, both India's and China's political and intelligence cooperation with the United States after the 9/11 terrorist attacks, India's democratic system, and China's critical geopolitical posture in Asia such as its role in defusing the North Korean nuclear crisis all make it easier for the two diasporas to lobby effectively in order to promote America's relations with the two Asian powers.

The Chinese-American community had long been labeled "a sleeping giant." Now, it's not only awake, but out of bed and standing up and is emerging as a political power not to be ignored.[8] Influential Chinese-American groups include the New York-based Committee of 100, which was founded in 1990 by famed architect I.M. Pei and renowned musician Yo-Yo Ma, and the Chinese American Voters Education Committee (CAVEC), which was formed in San Francisco Bay area to help Chinese Americans in national and local elections. The dual missions of the Committee of 100 are "to promote the full participation of Chinese-Americans in all fields of American life, and to encourage constructive relations between the people of the United States and Greater China."[9] Over the years the Committee of 100 has become an influential group that US policy makers seek to enlist for their own advantage. For example, in 1996 when the Committee of 100 announced its support for unconditional most-favored-nation (MFN) trade status for China, US Senator Bennett Johnston from Louisiana who had been working hard to promote human rights in China rushed to host a joint press conference to support the Committee's decision.[10]

In the 1980s a group of wealthy Indians who lived in America's affluent suburbs began to worry about the community's lack of political involvement. They set up such grass-roots organizations as the Indian American Forum for Political Education (IAFPE) in the late 1980s. Since then there has been a growing political lobby from Indian-American groups. The Virginia-based US India Political Action Committee (ISINPAC), set up at the end of 2001 and modeled on America Israel Political Action Committee (AIPAC), quickly attracted some 27,000 members and has established "excellent relationships with various influential American lobbying groups" and has become "a force to reckon with."[11] Partially due to strong lobbying activities by Indian-Americans, the India Caucus was formed in the House of Representatives in 1993. With over 175 members in the House of Representatives, the India Caucus became the largest of its kind in US Congress in 2003.[12] The US Senate established its own India Caucus in 2004.

Indian-Americans and Chinese-Americans have formed powerful lobbying groups to influence US policies towards their home countries. For example, during the 1999 Kargil conflict, Indian immigrants flooded congressional offices with emails urging speedy resolution. Later in a front-page report entitled "Activism Boosts India's Fortunes: Politically Vocal Immigrants Help Tilt Policy in Washington," *The Washington Post* noted, "Lawmakers complied and a few days later, in a White House meeting, Clinton cited Congressional pressure in urging (Pakistani Prime Minister) Sharif to withdraw his forces."[13] Similarly, ever since the so-called "engagement vs. containment" argument started, most Chinese-American groups have been firmly behind the engagement camp and have argued for improving relations between the two Pacific powers.

Analysis of findings i: what explains the similarities in the activities of chinese and indian diasporas?

Similarities may be explained by the following:

1) The economic law of supply and demand

From an economics perspective, activities of Chinese and Indian diaspora communities are clearly driven by the principle of supply and demand. On the supply side, non-resident Indians and overseas Chinese are relatively successful and wealthy immigrants in the West. On the demand side, both China and India are emerging powers seeking development and peaceful foreign relations. Any contributions--from direct investment to lobbying for favorable policies towards homeland--to these national goals are warmly welcome, including from diaspora groups.

2) Motivations

Like most other diaspora groups, many Chinese and Indians overseas are strongly identified with their ancestral homelands, even after they become naturalized citizens of their adopted countries. A striking similarity between Indian and Chinese diaspora communities is their strong nationalism and their influence on their host nations' foreign policy towards their motherland.

During the Cold War, denouncing communist Poland was a sure vote-getter in Chicago which has a large Polish-American population. In Miami, candidates have to practically demonize Fidel Castro and declare war on Cuba in order to win. But confronting China on issues like human rights won't win you votes in California. When the United States derailed Beijing's bid to host the 2000 Olympics, thousands of Bay area Chinese-Americans signed petitions in protest.[14] Similarly, in 1998 when India was condemned internationally for conducting nuclear tests, the Indian diaspora stood by India.[15]

In another example, Chinese-Americans are a major force in supporting the granting of MFN trade status to China during the 1990s. Even the Chinese-Americans most suspicious of Beijing—those from Taiwan—still overwhelmingly favor MFN (89 % in a Bay area poll by the Chinese language daily *Sing Tao*).[16] Many of these Chinese-Americans are well-positioned either to directly invest in China or to be sent to China by US companies in need of representatives with contacts and language skills.

Of course, in terms of motivations, when considering investment in their homeland, diasporas are also driven by material benefits. Like all business people, diasporas who invest in their homeland also want to make money. The huge markets, cheap labor and resources provide the necessary conditions for their activities in their homeland.

In addition, one cannot ignore the potential liberal role of diasporas in shaping the minds of people back home. Because of their familiarity with both cultures, diaspora groups play a special role in bridging their adopted country and ancestral country. Specifically, Indian and Chinese immigrants in the West can help bridge the gap between the East and the West. Through investment in education and infrastructure, for example, diasporas help to introduce or consolidate democratic cultures in their homelands.

Analysis of findings ii: what explains the differences in the activities of chinese and indian diaspora communities?

Differences in Indian and Chinese diaspora activities, summarized in Table 2, can be explained from several perspectives.

1) Historical differences

Arguably Chinese have a much longer history of traveling and living abroad than Indians. In the case of North America, Chinese laborers (coolies) helped build the trans-continental railway in the mid-19th century, earlier than any recorded large-scale Indian immigrants.

Chinese around the world are known for their business acumen. The Confucian virtue of thrift, discipline, industriousness, family cohesion, and reverence for education has positively contributed to the success of many overseas Chinese. Throughout history, Chinese living abroad have been attempting to help modernize their homeland. Overseas Chinese support and help of their homeland are duly admired and respected by people back home.

Table 2 Differences: A Tale of Two Diasporas

	Chinese-Americans	Indian-Americans
Historical	Long, Admired	Short, Resented
Cultural	"Fallen Leaves"	NRIs: "not required Indians"
Institutional	OCAO ACFROC	High Level Committee Pravasi Bharatiya Divas (PBD) Ministry of NRI

Economic model	FDI/export-oriented	Entrepreneurship /R&D
Geopolitical	Activities more constrained by US politics and policies	Activities less constrained by US politics and policies

Traditionally, overseas Chinese in Southeast Asia, due to their proximity to China proper and their successes in their countries of residence, form a major source of foreign direct investment in China. In more recent decades, wealthy Chinese in North America, Europe, Australia, and other developed regions have also invested heavily in China.

By contrast, the Indian diaspora was, at least until recently, resented for its success and much less willing to invest back home. India used to take a "dim view of Indians who had gone abroad".[17] NRIs (Non-resident Indians) used to be dubbed "not required Indians". Some were regarded as too poor to be bothered with. Those Indians who left during the British colonial rule were considered to be betraying and deserting their homeland. Those Indians who joined the brain drain of talent to the United States and other developed countries more recently were also viewed negatively.

Another major difference is that by the early 1980s when China began to open its economy to foreign investors, the Chinese in Hong Kong, Taiwan and Macao were already among the most successful exporters of labor-intensive manufacturers in the world. Unfortunately, the Indian diaspora apparently lacks this expertise, and there are no wealthy Indian diaspora-dominated regions or countries to provide such service.

2) Cultural differences

China has a large and wealthy diaspora that has long been eager to help the motherland, and its money has been warmly received. Cultural and family ties are a draw, along with a desire to give something back to the motherland. The "fallen leaves" are supposed to return to their roots when they get old. If they cannot physically return home, they would help families back home through remittances.

Due to its colonial experience, Indians used to regard foreign investment as an extension of the imperialist exploitation of local residents. Only in recent years has this mentality been slowly changing. After witnessing the sea changes in Shenzhen and the whole coastal region of China in the past two decades, the government of India is considering following China's footsteps and establishing some 20 special economic zones to attract more foreign direct investment and promote export.[18]

When comparing the social institutions and cultures in India and China and their readiness to absorb the mechanism of a market economy, a leading Chinese international relations scholar commented that India has a modern political structure, a basically modern economic structure, but its socio-cultural structure is pre-modern. Without a drastic social change like Maoist revolution in China, the blood or clan-centered social structure is incompatible with principles of the market economy.[19]

3) Institutional differences

Strong institutionalized links intimately connect China with overseas Chinese communities. Except during the Cultural Revolution, when people with overseas connections were looked down upon with suspicion, the Chinese government has been wooing overseas Chinese to contribute to the modernization of China. Since China opened its door again in the late 1970s, both official and societal attitudes toward overseas Chinese have changed. Overseas Chinese are admired and enthusiastically pursued by governments at all levels in China. The Chinese government has a special cabinet ministry to deal with overseas Chinese affairs. The Overseas Chinese Affairs Commission (OCAC) (*qiaowu weiyuanhui*), dissolved during the Cultural Revolution, was re-established in 1978 as the Overseas Chinese Affairs Office (*qiaowu bangongshi*). OCAC offices were also set up at provincial, municipal, county, and even some township and village levels all across China.

The All-China Federation of Returned Overseas Chinese (ACFROC) (*quanguo guiqiao lianhehui*) was also re-established in 1978 as a government-sanctioned mass organization to help returned overseas Chinese and their families.

In 1983, the National People's Congress, China's parliament, also formed a committee on overseas Chinese affairs. The main purpose of these institutions has been to encourage overseas Chinese to contribute to China's development.

China is a prime example of how a state has deliberately instituted policies to attract the resources of its diaspora in order to achieve rapid economic growth. These measures include establishing special economic zones, pass preferential laws, and use patriotic appeals. One example of a specific law for overseas Chinese is the "State Council's Regulation on Encouraging Overseas Chinese, Hong Kong, and Macao Compatriots to Invest in the Mainland," issued in 1990. Throughout the past two decades, the Chinese government has become more astute at attracting overseas Chinese. Government officials wine and dine potential investors, and more than 70 business parks have been set up exclusively for their use.[20]

By contrast, NRIs have long complained about their treatment by India. Corruption is a major issue. Whenever NRIs seek customs clearance, they are invariably pressured to pay bribes. There have been cases when NRI passengers were made to miss their flights because of callous officials. Indian-Americans also complain how difficult it is to donate money to worthwhile causes in India. The Foreign Contributions Regulation Act makes donations a nightmare of paper-work and corruption.[21] Up until the early 2000s, official policies regarding investment in India were still "damaging to the business climate," and obtaining an export license would require up to 250 official signatures.[22]

However, after decades of indifference, India has begun wooing its 20 million expatriates. The government of India established a High Level Committee on the India Diaspora in 2000 headed by Dr. L.M. Singhvi, MP, to study "the problems and difficulties, the hopes and expectations of the overseas Indian communities."[23] The committee, in its report to the Prime Minister, recommended that January 9, the day Mahatma Gandhi returned to India from South Africa in 1915, be celebrated as Pravasi Bharatiya Divas (Non-resident Indian Day). On January 9-11, 2003, the Indian government hosted its first ever gathering of global Indians in New Delhi. Prime Minister Atal Behari Vajpayee invited about 2,000 NRIs and others of Indian origin to the inaugural get-together. During the conference, India's Finance Minister announced substantial easing of overseas investment rules for both the private sector and individuals. Pravasi Bharatiya Divas has been institutionalized and become an annual event. India is also taking steps to grant dual citizenships for selected NRIs.

In addition, recognizing the importance and great potential of overseas Indians in India's development, in May 2004 a new government ministry—the Ministry of Overseas Indian Affairs (MOIA) was officially established by the Indian government. The new ministry is set up to help both NRIs and PIOs (person of Indian origins who have acquired citizenships of other countries) and their families on various issues such as investment safety, children's education, and employment of family members. Several years back, in its original proposal to set up the new ministry, the parliament's standing committee on external affairs claimed that NRIs and PIOs are "extremely valuable" to India's development.[24] Despite some bureaucratic and administrative delays, the new ministry seems to be seeking a bigger role in the political economy of India.[25] Since the power transition in India in the first half of 2004, the National Congress Party has continued to strengthen economic reforms including efforts to attract FDI.

4) Economic development models

Both Chinese and Indian economies were strongly influenced by the Soviet model which emphasized planning and industrialization. Mohandas Gandhi and Jawaharlal Nehru were two most influential men in modern Indian political economy. Yet the visions of the two for India were hardly alike: Gandhi believed India's future lay in self-reliant villages; but Nehru, influenced by Soviet socialism, wanted to urbanize and industrialize, filling India with steel mills, hydroelectric dams and engineering colleges.[26]

Nehru's vision won.

India did not adopt economic reforms until the early 1990s. Former Prime Minister Rajiv Gandhi brought the first supercomputer to India in 1990, and the Congress Party paved the way for the reforms that created the technology boom that have made cities like Bangalore and Hyderabad rivals of Silicon Valley. But it was also the Gandhi family that brought socialism to India, a system that created enormous regulatory barriers to businesses, both foreign and domestic.[27]

NRI remittances have influenced the Indian economy for many decades and since the economic liberalization in 1991, an even greater potential is seen in India's relations with the diaspora community. Between 1990 and 2000 remittances from abroad grew six-fold, from $2.1 billion to $12.3 billion.[28] This growth far exceeded growth in India's exports.

The different approaches to diaspora communities by India and China reflect their different economic development models. Chinese economic growth since the late 1970s has largely depended on foreign direct investment, and Chinese diaspora has contributed as much as 70% of total FDI. This helps explain why the Chinese government has vigorously pursued and attracted overseas Chinese to their ancestral homeland. India's economic reform has focused on restructuring indigenous traditional industries and developing new high-tech industries. The Indian government started to change policies to attract NRIs in the late 1990s. It can be expected that India will continue to appeal to the many high-tech industry-based NRIs in the hope of perhaps turning India into the world's technological lab much like overseas Chinese have helped turn China into the world's workshop.

5) Geopolitical differences

The different policies China and India adopt towards their diaspora communities also demonstrate the different political considerations of their governments. A major reason China has endeavored to attract overseas Chinese is that it needs to compete with Taiwan to win the hearts and minds of millions of ethnic Chinese around the globe. Indeed, Taiwan and the PRC each has a ministerial level office to handle overseas Chinese affairs. Winning sympathy and political support from overseas Chinese has been a major struggle between Taiwan and the PRC. By contrast, there is no such political incentive for India to enthusiastically woo its expatriates.

Lobbying competition between the PRC and Taiwan has become increasingly tense around the world since the early 1990s.[29] In the United States, the Taiwanese have a more sophisticated and longer history of lobbying. The annual debate in the US Congress over human rights and trade issues in China in the early 1990s made the Chinese government and many Chinese-Americans realize the importance of lobbying. Because of historical ties, shared values, and strong economic and strategic interests between Taiwan and the United States, the PRC government and its supporters face a tough job of garnering US support. Luckily for the PRC, the rising mainland market and its growing power and influence in world affairs greatly help stabilize relations between China and the United States. From the US perspective, China's increasing geopolitical influence, especially in the Asia Pacific region and on issues such as North Korea's nuclear crisis, makes it impossible for the US government to ignore China's interests promoted by Chinese-Americans and other groups who wish to maintain a stable relationship with China.

Indians in the United States are also rapidly acquiring political clout commensurate with their affluence. They are now poised to play the same role for their country of origin as other immigrant groups such as the Jewish community has been to Israel. Not long ago, India was almost subjected to economic sanctions by the US Congress for perceived violations of civil rights in Jammu, Kashmir and Punjab, but now the situation is very different. In 1998, the Congress passed legislation diluting sanctions imposed by President Bill Clinton after India's nuclear tests. In its 107th session the US Congress passed a resolution supporting a permanent seat for India in the UN Security Council. In another example, Ms Shirin Tahir-Kheli was considered as a front-runner to succeed Mr. Karl Inderfurth as the New Assistant Secretary for South Asian Affairs. The Assistant Secretary for South Asia is a key figure in steering US policies towards the region. Some members of the Indian-American community launched an email-blitz to voice their concern at Ms. Tahir-Kheli's close Pakistani connections. Finally, Ms. Christina Rocca was appointed the Assistant Secretary for South Asia and Ms. Kheli, the head of the US delegation to the UN Commission on Human Rights.[30]

It must be mentioned that Pakistanis in the United States have also been lobbying "at a frenetic pace" in recent years, especially with focus on the Kashimir issue to win the support of the United States.[31] But Pakistani-American lobbying has not proved a formidable challenge to the more experienced and better-organized Indian-American lobbying.

Due to different political systems in India and China, Indian-American lobbying activities are less constrained by American politics than Chinese-Americans. Democratic values sell well in America. In the wake of 9/11, a democracy like India or Israel can effectively present an image of a peace-loving democracy being threatened by terrorists, and receive moral, political and military support from the United States.

In recent years Indian-Americans and Jewish-Americans have successfully teamed up to push for US policies favorable to their homelands. For example, in the summer of 2003, pro-Israel and pro-India groups successfully worked together to gain the Bush administration's approval for Israel to sell four Phalcon early warning radar planes to India for about $1 billion, a deal that has alarmed the Pakistani government. Three years earlier, the United States government blocked a nearly identical proposal that Israel sell radar planes to China.[32] During President Bush's South Asia trip in March 2006, the United States reached a historic agreement to share nuclear reactors, fuel and expertise with India. Meanwhile, the United States still maintains export controls to China as part of the economic sanctions against China that were first imposed following the Tiananmen Square incident in 1989. The logic behind all these is simple: Unlike China, India is a democracy and is unlikely to threaten America's national interests. India is also increasingly perceived by some in the United States as a counterweight against the rising Chinese power.

Concluding Remarks

In various ways diaspora communities maintain close contact with their ancestral homelands. An issue that has not been systematically investigated is the role these diaspora groups play in the political economy of their homelands. This research has attempted to fill the theoretical and policy gap in this area. The findings suggest that Indian and Chinese diasporas in the United States have contributed positively to the economic development of their ancestral homelands and promoted relations between their countries of origin and countries of residence. The findings also suggest that the significant roles of Indian and Chinese diasporas in their respective homelands' development and foreign relations consistently reflect, and are strongly influenced by, economic development strategies as well as political history and culture of their homelands. The comparison of Chinese-Americans and Indian-Americans indicates that the extent to which diasporas can promote relations between their homeland and country of residence is constrained by the state of bilateral relations between the two countries. The findings appear to confirm the validity of the two hypotheses proposed earlier. The examination of Chinese and Indian diaspora activities also provides a new perspective in the study of the political economy of China and India.

Chinese and Indians are considered two of the major "global tribes" who have achieved economic success in contemporary international political economy.[33] The state-diaspora interactions will only become more active in the global economy of the 21st century. Globalization will deepen and widen the process of international migration since it promotes the movements of capital, commodities, personnel, and cultures across national borders. The traditional "brain drain" from developing countries to the Western world has already been replaced by "brain circulation," meaning a variety of two-way flows of highly skilled workers between the technologically advanced countries where they reside and the less-developed countries where they were born, especially in the case of Chinese and Indian professionals in North America.[34] This has become a unique phenomenon in contemporary international political economy. Since these diaspora communities clearly exert social, cultural, political and economic impact on the developments of both India and China, their international roles need to be more closely examined.

The comparative study of Chinese and Indian diasporas also raises questions for further research. Up till now, China has done a better job than India in obtaining the support of overseas Chinese for China's economic growth, and yet China is not a democracy. Students of political systems may ask: Does regime type matter? Or perhaps government policies, not government types, are more relevant in this situation? What implications does the study of Chinese and Indian diasporas have for other developing countries?

The rise of the twin powers of China and India in the 21st century will certainly affect America's interests in and policies towards Asia. The lobbying power of Chinese-Americans and Indian-Americans and its consequences cannot be overlooked by American policy makers and the public. And finally, since many diasporas have lived in the West for years, and many have become permanent residents or citizens, they may face issues of national identity and loyalty, which also directly concerns immigration, social and other policies of the West. If diasporas do play a significant role in the political economy and foreign relations of their countries of origin, then clearly Western countries need to pay more attention to these residents within their borders when attempting to expand and strengthen relations with other countries, including India and China.

Notes

[1] Diaspora, as used in this article, includes both those who live out of their homeland temporarily and those who have already acquired citizenship of their country of residence but remain strongly attached to their country of origin. The Chinese diaspora is commonly known as overseas Chinese, and the Indian diaspora is officially called Non-resident Indians. The Indian figure is from India's Ministry of External Affairs. See "Non Resident Indians & Persons of Indian Origin Division, Ministry of External Affairs, New Delhi, India," at <http://indiandiaspora.nic.in>. The Chinese figure is from various sources.

[2] According to Merrill Lynch figures, there are 200,000 Indian millionaires in the U.S., or about one in 10 of all Indian immigrants to the U.S. See Prasad, Sunil, "Can the Indian Diaspora Help India Overtake China?" Global Organization of People of India Origin (GOPIO) paper, accessed online from <www.gopio.net/India_China_0703.doc>. See also, "Never Mind China, Watch India," *The Toronto Star*, April 28, 2004, accessed online from <www.thestar.com> the same day. [3] For a detailed discussion of these theories, see for example, Laurence J. C. Mar and Carolyn Cartier (eds.) *The Chinese Diaspora* (Lanham, Maryland: Rowman & Littlefield Publishers, Inc., 2003).

[4] See, for example, Sunil Prasad, "Can the Indian Diaspora Help India Overtake

China?" Global Organization of People of India Origin (GOPIO) paper, accessed online from <www.gopio.net/India_China_0703.doc>; and Sadananda Sahoo, "Can India Catch Up With China? From a Diaspora Perspective," Center for the Study of Indian Diaspora, University of Hyderabad, September 2002, accessed online at <http://www.geocities.com/husociology/china.htm>.

5. It is generally believed that direct and indirect investment from Chinese in Hong Kong, Macao, and Taiwan is included in the calculation. According to the "round-tripping" hypothesis, mainland Chinese firms transfer funds to Hong Kong, Macao, Taiwan, and other regions and then re-invest in China as FDI inflows in order to benefit from the preferential treatment. Estimates suggest that round-tripping FDI accounts for one-fourth of China's total FDI. See Nirupam Bajpai and Nandita Dasgupta, "FDI to China and India: The Definitional Differences," *Business Line* (internet edition), May 15, 2004 at www.thehindubusinnesline.com/ 2004/05/15/stories/ 2004051500081000.htm.

6. "Didn't They Do Well? The diaspora is 'discovered,'" *The Economist*, January 25, 2003: p. 44.

7. This paper focuses on diaspora's contributions to homeland's development in terms of investment. Without doubt, their contributions are multidimensional including, for example, setting up schools and training centers, building bridges and hospitals, and simply introducing Western management and business culture to their homeland.

8. "Chinese Americans Emerge as a Political Power in S.F.," *The Los Angeles Times*, February 1, 2004, accessed online from <www.latimes.com> on February 2, 2004.

9. See the Committee's website at <www.committee100.org>.

10. Peter Beinart, "Domestic Partners: China's codependents in the U.S.," *The New Republic,* March 10, 1997: p. 15.

11. "Indian-Americans No Longer on the Political Sidelines," *Daily Times* (Pakistan), December 22, 2003. Accessed online from <www.dailytimes.com.pk> on February 2, 2004.

12. Ibid.

13. *The Washington Post*, October 9, 1999.

14. Beinart, "Domestic Partners," p. 14.

15. Prasad, Sunil, "Can the Indian Diaspora Help India Overtake China?" Global Organization of People of India Origin (GOPIO) paper, accessed online from <www.gopio.net/India_China_ 0703.doc>.

16. Beinart, "Domestic Partners," p. 14.

17. Yasheng Huang and Tarun Khanna, "Can India Overtake China?" *Foreign Policy* (July/August 2003), p. 75

18. The Indian Elephant Catches up Quickly with the Chinese Dragon," *Lianhe Zaobao (Singapore),* accessed online at <www.zaobao.com> on January 25, 2004.

19. Ibid.

20. "On Their Way Back," *The Economist*, November 6, 2003.

21. "The Indian American Diaspora—How it contributes towards India," *Business Line*,

22 August 7, 2002.
23 David Masci, "Emerging India: Current Situation," *CQ Researcher*, April 19, 2002, pp. 346-349.
24 Quoted from India's Ministry of External Affairs website on the Indian Diaspra at <http://indiandiaspora.nic.in>.
25 "Ministry to Set up Department to Deal with Woes of NRIs," *Press Trust of India*, April 22, 2000. "Allot Work to NRI: Parliamentary Panel," *Indo-Asian News Service*, August 25, 2004.
26 "The Man Who Made India," *Time (Asia Edition),* December 8, 2003, Vol 162, No 22.
27 "Can Gandhi Heirs Revive Dynasty?" *The Christian Science Monitor*, January 30, 2004: p. 6.
28 "The Indian American Diaspora—How it contributes towards India," *Business Line*, August 7, 2002.
29 For a detailed account of the PRC-Taiwan lobbying competition see Zhiqun Zhu's "Battle Without Gunfire: Taiwan and the PRC's Lobbying Competition in the United States" in *Asian Perspective*, Vol. 24, No. 1 (2000), pp. 47-70.
30 "The Indian American Diaspora—How it contributes towards India," *Business Line*, August 7, 2002.
31 See for example, "Expat Paks Intensify Lobbying in Washington," *The Rediff News,* June 18, 1998, accessed online from <http://www.rediff.com/news/1998/jun/18bomb.htm>.
32 Alan Cooperman, "India, Israel Interests Team Up," *The Washington Post*, July 19, 2003.
33 According to Joel Kotkin, the other "global tribes" include the Jews, the British, and Japanese. See Kotkin, *Tribes: How Race, Religion, and Identity Determine Success in the New Global Economy* (New York: Random House, 1993).
34 Moises Naim, "The New Diaspora," *Foreign Policy,* July/August 2002.

3

Indian Overseas Organization from Canada, Promoting Hindi, Sanskrit and Indian Culture in the world.

Sunita Narale[2]

Competing with the wild spread of English Language and Culture in the world, Pustak Bharati (Books-India) of Toronto is the only organization from Canada, that is promoting and spreading Hindi, Sanskrit and Indian culture in the whole world, through its vast book publication, educational classes, e-Journalism and e-lessons. It is not an exaggeration but it is a fact because, outside India there probably is no individual or an organization that has published as many precious books, publications and journals and made available in the world through amazon.com to promote Hindi, Sanskrit, Indian Culture, Gita, Ramayan, Yoga and other Indian Languages, as Pustak Bharati had done and is doing. Over last 50 years Pustak Bharati has taught Hindi, Sanskrit and Gita to virtually thousands of students, young and old.

As they say, steel cuts steel. Following the same principle, making use of the wide spread and the power of the English language, Pustak Bharati is using English medium in the English speaking world to effectively promote Hindi and Indian culture in the entire world since at least 20 years to convert English Speaking people into Hindi Speaking and Hindi loving.

Teaching Hindi through Hindi medium, writing Hindi poetry, stories and books,

---

[2] Sunita Narale, Freelance writer, Toronto, Canada

conducting Hindi poetic meets and groups are all nice, useful and enjoyable, but only for those who already know Hindi. However, how about those English speaking Indian Diaspora from Mauritius, Guyana, Trinidad and Tobago, Surinam, Fiji and all other countries in the world and the English speaking descendents of Indian people living outside India and those millions of non-Indian English speaking people who have purpose or interest in Indian languages and culture? How do we educate, connect and integrate these wonderful people into our Hindi loving chain. And how do we pass on this wealth to their future generations con come?

Pustak Bharati firmly believes that sowing seeds of Hindi in Non-Hindi speaking people everywhere is the most valuable and everlasting service we can give to this world so that then through the new recruits Hindi will grow and grow for ever with compounded interest. We follow the proverb, "if you feed a fish to a person, he is satisfied for a day only, but if you teach him how to catch a fish, he is set for lifetime and he will teach that skill to many people, and the art will grow non-stop."

Normally, the main activity of the individuals and organizations engaged in the promotion of Hindi is to gather weekly, monthly, quarterly, yearly or occasionally to hold Hindi poetic meets, Hindi conventions, Hindi drama, singing Hindi songs, Hindi book club, Hindi book release, Hindi discussions, picnics, and to provide a stage for other wonderful activities. Also, another activity is to publish a periodical Hindi Magazine to publish Hindi poems and stories from various Hindi writers for the recreation of Hindi Bhashi readers in the name of Service to Hindi Bhasha. They are all nice, but they provide benefit, recreation and pastime for time being only. On the contrary, Pustak Bharati is dedicated to teach Hindi in classes and online; produce, publish and distribute books online and sow the seeds of Hindi, Indian culture, Gita, Ramayan, Yoga, Indian Music, Indian arts and Indian languages in order to bond people around the world with Indian culture through English medium for English Speaking People and in Hindi Medium for Hindi Bhashi People in the name of service to Hindi Bhasha and for the Hindi Bhashi people. We distinction between the services of narrow scope for Hindi Bhashi People and the service of wide scope for the Hindi Bhasha.

With the objectives of the service to Hindi Bhasha and to Hindi Bhashi people, Pustak Bharati is dedicated to develop new techniques to produce educational books for teaching how to read-write-speak Hindi and various other Indian Languages on one hand and on the other hand publish, print and distribute literature on poetry-prosody-music, Sanskrit-Sanskriti-Sanskar, Gita-Ramayan-Yoga for English and Hindi Bhashi people in he world. In these activities Pustak Bharati, entertainment may be less, but these value added services have everlasting benefit.

Now let us take a brief look at the history and practical examples of the precious achievements of the Pustak Bharati over last fifty years in Canada. Pustak Bharati was initiated in Toronto Canada in 1969, as an unofficial and unregistered body by a group of crazy individuals whose aim was to spread Indian Culture, National Language, Sanskrit and Indian Music in Canada. The group was joined by equally dedicated Diaspora from Guyana, Trinidad, Fiji, Mauritius and Surinam.

In those days there wee no computers. All manuscript writing had to be handwritten or typewritten material. Typewritten manuscripts had to be in Romanized English or on a crude Devanagari typewriter. Copies had to be made by cyclostyle or blueprinting, with handmade binding and with such booklets we had to run Hindi, Sanskrit and Gita classes.

Then came Xerox machines and our quality and speed increased significantly. Our books became popular. Even then typewriter being the only device, the quality of the books was very poor. The work was slow, but there was no alternative.

Then came IBM computers, Data Processing Softwares, CD ROM equipment, and out efficiency and speed rocketed high. Pustak Bharati became a registered company and under the name of PC PLUS Ltd. Publishing Copy write plus printing and distribution work began. The company began producing its own Devanagari Data Processing Personal Computers. It produced Hindi-Sanskrit-Marathi fonts. Then Tamil, Punjabi and Urdu fonts were added. Pustak Bharati then began designing and developing Phonetically Color Coded Alphabet Charts. They became excellent learning/teaching tools. Institutions and students made extensive use of them. Then came Hindi Learning and Hindi typing CDs. They were bundled with our Hindi Learning Books. Our

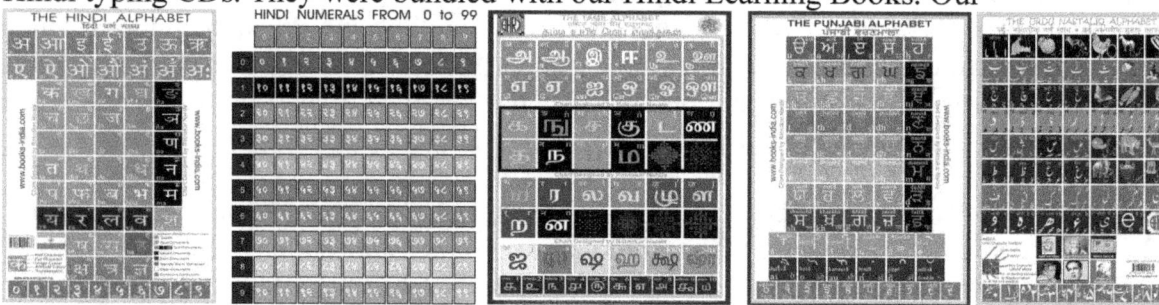

language learning charts were a great attraction for the schools and temples teaching Indian languages.

These charts were a priceless gift for the serious students and many institutes prepared large posters to put in the Hindi and Sanskrit classes for the help of the students. These unique charts designed after long research and development work, are the best phonetical and scientific like of which do not exist anywhere. Color coded in theses charts is complete phonetical and grammatical information such as Root vowels and consonants with their English equivalents, Compound vowels and consonants, Semi consonants, Half consonants, Full consonants, Nasal consonants, Class consonants, non-class consonants, Hard consonants, Soft consonants, Warm consonants, Aspirate consonants, Classification according to the shape of the consonants, writing flow of each alphabet, etc.

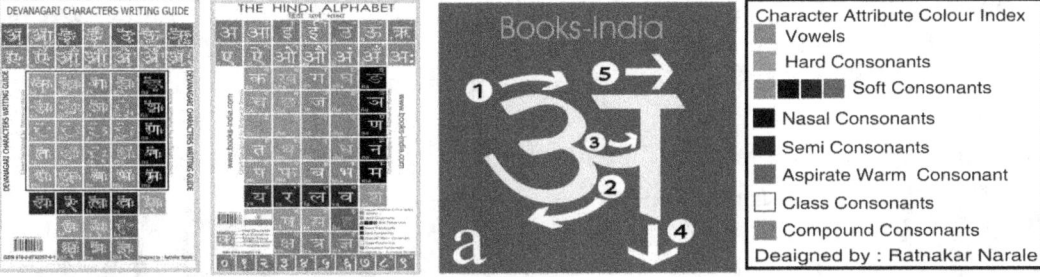

Then came out the Hindi Learning CD for those students who could not attend classes and wanted to learn Hindi on their own without the help of a teacher. Later on the 3 CDs and the 2 Devanagari charts were bundled with the Hindi Learning books as a complete kit for the student out of town and out of Canada in the world. Our main two Devanagari fonts are "Sarasvati" and "Ratnakar" ttf fonts. The fonts are so beautiful and ornate that news media, publishers, authors and students loved them. The keyboard layout is exactly same as QWERTY English keyboard and thus quick and natural to learn and adopt. The fonts are superior as each character and symbol is carefully designed so that even in very small size they are easily legible. The letters are neither too dark nor too faint. It should have all punctuation, typographic and also Indian musical symbols and accent marks built in the font. And most precious thing for the Sanskrit scholars is that one can type most complicated Sanskrit compound letters such as dbra, dgra, ndvi, nkhya, nkshya, ngkta, ngu, etc. properly, without using of halant matra and without being a novice. Hindi Unicode font users have become so much used to typing and reading crudely typed Sanskrit and Hindi text that many of them don't even know the difference, what is proper and what is improper. Fee the following short illustration, for example :

ड्रि	ध्दि	न्द्वि	ह्ण	ह्न	ह्म	ह्य	ह्ल	ह्व	इक्त	इख	इघ	इल	इक्षि	इक्ष्व	इम
इगि	दयि	न्दवि	हण	हन	हम	हय	हल	हव	इक्त	इख	इघ	इल	इक्षि	इक्ष्व	इम

One of the happy user of these fonts Mr. Sunny Bass writes, *"Hello Ratnakarji, the your font is really nice and clear, probably the nicest one I have ever seen."* And as a result, on popular demands we designed and created custom fonts. We designed and developed "Adesh" font for Prof. Hari Shankar Adesh, the first winner of Padmabhushan Dr Moturi Satyanarayana Award; "Rakaesh" font for Hindi Times Media; "Ganeshji" font for Hindi Abroad; "ST" font for Hindi Chetna; "Sharda" font for Hindu Institute; "Canada" font for the Hanuman Mandir; "Neil, Sunil and Music" fonts for Academy of Indian Music, "Ratnakar" font for typesetting over 80 Sanskrit-Hindi books of Prof. Ratnakar Narale, "Sarasvati" font for author Dr. Sushila Devi Gupta for many of her Hindi/Sanskrit books, and many more.

In 1989 came World Wide Web and Pustak Bharati designed its own website to make

available wonderful and colorful Free Online Hindi Lessons for the students and Hindi learners across the world. These free and priceless lessons became so popular that the website had over a million visitors per year. The name Pustak Bharati became a household popular word well beyond the borders of Canada, in the English speaking areas of the whole world. It also increased the popularity of the Hindi Learning book that optionally went hand in hand along with the online lessons.

On January 10, 1991 Pustak Bharati became a registered organization. It began writing scholarly books for the higher studies of Sanskrit and Gita. On January 10, 2006 it received ISBN issuing authority from the Library and Archives of Government of

Canada. It then became a member of the Amazon Group and published and distributed over 60 of its quality books on www.amazon.com and now available through amazon.in and amazon.uk also. Pustak Bharati has sold thousands of its wonderful books to the students, scholars, teachers, professors and the lovers of Bharatiya Sanskriti in almost every country of the world and has done a great service in teaching and promoting Hindi, Sanskrit, Gita, Ramayan and Music.

A Ph.D. scholar of IIT Kharagpur, India, the CEO of Pustak Bharati and Editor-in-Chief  of Pustak Bharati Research Journal, Toronto, Canada and Pradhanacharya of Hindu Institute, Toronto, Canada, Prof. Ratnakar Narale has Ph.D. from Kalidas Sanskrit University, Nagpur, India also. He chairs Sanskrit Study Circle in Toronto. He is living in Toronto for over 50 years and has won many National and International awards. He has taught Hindi in all three Universities of Toronto, both the School Boards of the greater Toronto, private Institutions, home classes and produced virtually thousands of students over last 50 years. He has written over 60 books to promote Indian Culture. Many of the books are award winners and they are popular in the four corners of the world. Thanks to amazon.com.

Dr. Rakesh Kumar Dubey, (M.A., NET, Ph.D.) BHU, Varanasi, India is the Sub-Editor of  the Pustak Bharati Research Journal. He has written over 80 research papers and articles for reputed journals from India and abroad, such as 'Whitaker Science Award, 2012' Vijyan Parishad, Prayagraj, U.P., India, Hindi Essay writing Award, 2015, WHS, Mauritius. He has participated in over 30 International/National seminars and presented papers. He has won many Research and Post Doctoral fellowships. He is the well known author of 'Bharatiya Rashtriya Aandolan men Kashi ki Nagaripracharini Sabha ka Yogdan." This dynamic scholar has association with the scholars and professionals from over 25 countries in the world.

Now let us take a look at some of the Pustak Bharati's popular books

पुस्तक भारती कनाडा की amazon.com एवं amazom.in पर उपलब्ध पुस्तकें, हैपर-लिंक के साथ
email : pustak.bharati.canada@gmail.com * Web : www.pustak-bharati-canada.com

हिंदी पुस्तकें

| Cover | Title / Author | ISBN / Cover | No. Pages | Discretion |

Sunita Narale

	बालकृष्ण दोहावली Ratnakar Narale	978-1897416945 Soft Cover	198	व्रजभूमि के पार्श्व में रचे हुए इस छंदकाव्य में व्रजवासी जीवन के पहलुओं के रंगभरे मनोरम सप्राण वर्णन प्रस्तुत हैं. व्रजवासी समस्याओं का निरूपण व निराकरण इसकी एक विशेषता है.
	नंदकिशोर दोहावली Ratnakar Narale	978-1897416952 Soft Cover	122	वृंदावन की कुंज गलिन में राधा-नंदकिशोर की अमर लीलाएँ और उस पुरातन काल के ग्रामीण परिवेश की प्रस्तुति व मधुबन का जीता-जागता ग्रामीण वर्णन प्रदर्शित किया गया है.
	संगीत गीता दोहावली Ratnakar Narale	978-1897416860 Soft Cover	572	नए सिरे से शत प्रतिशत अनुष्टुभ छंद में लिखी हुई यह विश्व की पहली भगवद्गीता है. रिसर्च स्कॉलर्स के लिए नूतन विषयों का अथाह सागर है.
	संगीत रामायण दोहावली Ratnakar Narale	978-1897416938 Soft Cover	630	ग्रामीण अवधी संस्कृति के हर एक पहलू के सूक्ष्म संगीतमय वर्णन से आरंभ होकर राम-सीता के अयोध्या से लंका तक ग्राम्य सांस्कृतिक विवरण के सजीव वर्णन का सुंदर व मंगल दर्शन है.
	शिवाजी चरित्र दोहावली Ratnakar Narale	978-1897416303 Soft Cover	452	यह ऐतिहासक महाकविता छत्रपति शिवाजी के अद्भुत शिवलीलामृत है. इस के तीन सहस्र दोहों में और एक शत से अधिक राष्ट्रभक्ति हिंदी गीतों में राष्ट्रप्रेम ओतप्रोत भरा हुआ है.

Sunita Narale

	Title	ISBN / Format	Price	Description
	भारतीय राष्ट्रीय आंदोलन और काशी की नागरीप्रचारिणी सभा डा. राकेश कुमार दूबे,	978-1897416877 Soft Cover	320	काशी नागरीप्रचारिणी सभा के बहआयामी कार्यों पर विस्तृत प्रकाश डाला गया है। सभा ने आम जनता द्वारा व्यवहृत हिंदी भाषा और नागरी लिपि का प्रचार और उसी के माध्यम से संपूर्ण देश को एकसूत्र में बांधते का प्रयास किया।
	हिंदी साहित्य का काव्यात्मक इतिहास रजनी सिंह	978-1897416983 Soft Cover	184	composed with an objective to offer sufficient knowledge of Hindi literature to present graduate students research scholars and lovers of Hindi language and those who are pursuing education in Hindi literature, in Universities of the World
	प्रेरणा पथ पंकज जाधव	978-1897416921 Soft Cover	130	किशोरावस्था से युवावस्था में प्रवेश करने वाले छात्र तथा छात्रों के सही मार्गदर्शन के लिए उनके उज्ज्वल भविष्य की कामना के लिए यह किताब लिखी गयी है। बातों-बातों में छात्रों की समझ तक पहुँचाने का प्रयत्न "प्रेरणा पथ" के माध्यम से किया गया है।
	संगीत श्री-रामायण प्रो. रत्नाकर नराले,	978-1897416907 Soft Cover	1200	श्रीराम चंद्र की अद्भुत लीलाओं से भरा हुआ यह आध्यात्मिक गहनता से परिपूर्ण चरित्र जागतिक इतिहास में अनुपम है। यह ज्ञान वर्धक, भक्ति दायक, शद्धि कारक, मनोरंजक, सुंदर, पवित्र, प्रेरणा दायक, पठनीय, ज्ञातव्य, मननीय, संग्रहणीय है।
	संगीत श्री-कृष्णायन Ratnakar Narale	9781897416891 Soft Cover	1086	World's first Opera-musical Style epic mega poem of *Sangit-Shri-Krishnayan* in the form of 100 short musical stories, plus their side stories, illustrates the wonderful, amusing, inspirational, educational and divine deeds of Shri Krishna

Sunita Narale

Book	ISBN / Cover	Price	Description
संगीत-श्रीकृष्ण-रामायण गीतमाला के गिने-चुने पुष्प Ratnakar Narale	978-1897416020 Soft Cover	130	संगीत-श्रीकृष्णायन तथा संगीत-श्रीरामायण के अंतर्गत गिने-चुने गानों का सुंदर संग्रह. संगीत सीखने एवं सिखाले के लिए मनोरंजक, स्फ़ूर्तिदायक और भक्तिपूर्ण साधन.
गीता का शब्दकोश और अनुक्रमणी प्रो. रत्नाकर नराले,	978-1897416648 Soft Cover	445	Gita Ka Shabdakosh, New Edition, is a systematically laid out one-of-a-kind All-in-one Gita-Dictionary, Gita-Grammar, Gita-Thesaurus, Gita-Reference, Gita-Index and much more, in Devanagari Sanskrit-Hindi.
संगीत श्री सत्यनारायण व्रत कथा प्रो. रत्नाकर नराले,	978-1897416839 Soft Cover	102	The new musical Stories of Shri-Satya-Narayan Vrat are composed by Ratnakar and presented along with the divine stories narrated by Bhagavan Vyas Muni, in the Reva Khand of the Skand Puran.
प्रज्ञा पुराण ज्ञानामृतम् डा. सुशीला देवी गुप्ता	978-1897416709 Hard Cover	260	This work is based on Dr. Sushila Devi's thesis submitted to the Meerut University for degree of D. Lit. It has ancient traditions of the Vedas, Brahmanas, Upanishads, Vedangas, Darshans, Sutras, Mahabharat and the puranas in simple language.
छात्रोपयोगी गीता डा. सुशीला देवी गुप्ता	978-1897416730 Soft Cover	266	Chhatropayogi Gita is tailored to introduce the average readers to the divine message of the Gita with interesting stories and songs, in the form of innovative Student-Teacher dialogues.

Sunita Narale

संगीत-श्रीकृष्ण-रामायण खंड-2

प्रो. रत्नाकर नराले,

9781897416815
Hard Cover

912

इसमें अनेक नैतिक, आध्यात्मिक व प्रेरणात्मक दृष्टान्तों के साथ साथ संगीत की अनेक राग रागनियोंसे परिपूर्ण विभिन्न रंग की छटा दिखाकर सब को सम्मोहित कर रहे हैं ।

संगीत-श्रीकृष्ण-रामायण खंड-1

प्रो. रत्नाकर नराले,

978-1897416433
Hard Cover

740

श्री कृष्ण की कथाऔं का इतना सुंदर, मधुर, सव्यवस्थित और संगीतमय वर्णन अन्यत्र कहीं नहीं मिलेगा । इसमें आदि से अन्त तक ज्ञान, कर्म व भक्ति त्रिवेणी प्रवाहित है ।

Hindi Language Learning Books

Hindi Teacher for Hindu Children

प्रो. रत्नाकर नराले,

9781897416570
Soft Cover

248

The book begins with simple primary steps and moves forward with authentic examples coupled with Progressive Exercises suitable to each context to bring home the topic being discussed. You will not find such contemplative and innovative work in any Hindi learning book.

Hindi Teacher for Hindu Children
Color Coded Edition

प्रो. रत्नाकर नराले,

9781897416754
Soft Cover

310

Language is the path way to the culture. Children are our precious wealth and our future. They need to be taught our lofty Hindu Values in a fun filled manner. While teaching the Hindi language, our children must be enlightened in the glorious Hindu Dharma.

Hindi Teacher for English Speaking People

प्रो. रत्नाकर नराले,

9781897416600
Soft Cover

194

This methodical book is based on extensive R&D, Effective Techniques and Improved Ways beneficial to the Readers to give them proper reture for their investment of Time and Money.

Sunita Narale

	Hindi Teacher for English Speaking People Colour Coded Edition प्रो. रत्नाकर नराले,	9781897416600 Soft Cover	254	The Vocabulary and Illustrations are selected carefully to offer a window to the topics, as used in Real Life Situations. It also has Hindi learners' Transliterated and intelligently color coded HINDI-ENGLISH DICTIONARY.
	Hindi Teacher for English Speaking People, Advanced Leve प्रो. रत्नाकर नराले,	9781897416617 Soft Cover	283	This book for those who have a basic knowledge of Hindi. It gives a comprehensive intro to Hindi music, Hindi writers and Hindi literature from the ancient to the modern times. It also has a fully transliterated Students Hindi English Dictionary.

संस्कृत पुस्तकें

	रत्नाकर-रचितम् गीतोपनिषद् (संस्कृत) प्रो. रत्नाकर नराले,	978-1897416853 Soft Cover	584	It is world's first Sanskrit rendering of the Gita, wholly in *Anushtubh Shloka chhanda* of Valmiki.
	Sanskrit Primer प्रो. रत्नाकर नराले,	9781897416556 Soft Cover	204	The step-by-step progress of this book gives the reader a high degree of success. It is a treasure of new ideas, techniques, information and reference material. It is rich with examples, exercises and an important chapter of "Answers to all the Exercises."
	Sanskrit Primer, Colour Coded प्रो. रत्नाकर नराले,	978-1897416914 Soft Cover	186	This color coded edition. It systematically laid out **Five Star** book with the best reviews, is*fully transliterated* for the benefit of the new learners of Sanskrit language.

Title	ISBN / Cover	Price	Description
Sanskrit Teacher All in One Soft Cover प्रो. रत्नाकर नराले,	9781897416549 Soft Cover	710	This ocean of jewels, created with extensive R&D, is worth its weight in gold. This unique book is Transliterated, in addition to the Sanskrit Script, for the benefit of English readers.
Sanskrit Teacher, All-In-One Without transliteration Hard Cover प्रो. रत्नाकर नराले,	9781897416792 Hard Cover	634	This giant 600 page All-in-One book (37 Chapters + 10 large Appendices) is for all levels of Sanskrit Self Learning for a novice as well as an expert.
Sanskrit Grammar and Reference Book Hard Cover प्रो. रत्नाकर नराले,	9781897416686 Hard Cover	686	A must for Sanskrit students, this book is one of its kind, worth its weight in gold. The question is not, "can you afford to buy it," the question is "can you afford not to buy this priceless book?"
Sanskrit for English Speaking People, Colour Coded Edition प्रो. रत्नाकर नराले,	9781897416747 Soft Cover	468	It is a step-by-step teaching and self-learning tool to read, write, understand and speak Sanskrit. This book is suited for beginner to intermediate level learners.
Yoga Sutras of Patanjali, Made Easy प्रो. रत्नाकर नराले,	9781897416532 Soft Cover	180	Each word is analyzed and transliterated to make learning of Yoga Sutras easy. The subject is analysed under 90 unique subheadings. The definitions and indices make a valuable reference guide.

Sunita Narale

Yoga Sutras of Patanjali, with Asana Steps, Colour Coded Edition
प्रो. रत्नाकर नराले,

9781897416884
Soft Cover

268

Definations of the Yogis terms and the detailed subject classification of all the sutras is the unique feature of this book. Sutra Index and Asana steps are the special additions for the help of the yoga students.

गीता पठनम्
प्रो. रत्नाकर नराले,

9781897416198
Soft Cover

Shlokas of the Bhagavad Gita are arranged in 8 syllable sections and two columns for proper singing and recitation. The text is printed in bigger size Devanagari Sanskrit Font for comfortable reading.

OTHER LANGUAGES LEARNING BOOKS

Gurumukhi Teacher
ਗੁਰਮੁਖੀ ਟੀਚਰ
प्रो. रत्नाकर नराले,

9781897416761
Soft Cover

This book is effective in results and easy for use. You will not find such contemplative and innovative work in any Punjabi-Gurumukhi learning book.

Tamil Teacher
தமிழ் ஆசிரியர்
प्रो. रत्नाकर नराले,

9781897416587
Soft Cover

It is fully English transliterated for your help. It is also coupled with Devanagari script for those who know Hindi or Sanskrit.

Urdu Teacher
اردو استاد
प्रो. रत्नाकर नराले,

9781897416662
Soft Cover

192

It is a step-by-step learning fully English transliterated for your help. It is also coupled with Devanagari script for those who understand India's National Language Hindi.

GITA BOOKS

Sunita Narale

	Title	ISBN / Cover	Pages	Description
	Gita as She Is, in Krishna's Own Words, Volume I प्रो. रत्नाकर नराले,	978-1897416112 Hard Cover	366	This is a critical research work. It is a lifetime study to learn and contemplate on the divine Gita. To learn or teach Gita through Sanskrit and Sanskrit through Gita, there is no substitute.
	Gita as She Is, in Krishna's Own Words, Volume II प्रो. रत्नाकर नराले,	9781897416501 Hard Cover	432	The footnotes in this book open your eyes to realize the misconceptions and wrong notions you have collected without properly knowing what the Sanskrit words of Krishna truly mean.
	Gita as She Is, in Krishna's Own Words, Volume III प्रो. रत्नाकर नराले,	9781897416693 Hard Cover	225	Regardless of how many books on Gita you may have read, studied or written, while going through this treasure of information, you will discover many Surprises, Interesting facts and Important points.
	संगीत गीता दोहावली प्रो. रत्नाकर नराले,	978-1897416860 Soft Cover	572	नए सिरे से शत प्रतिशत अनुष्टुभ छंद में लिखी हुई यह विश्व की पहली भगवद्गीता है. यह रिसर्च स्कॉलर्स के लिए नूतन विषयों का अथाह सागर है.
	गीता का शब्दकोश और अनुक्रमणी प्रो. रत्नाकर नराले,	9781897416648 Soft Cover	445	*Gita Ka Shabdakosh, New Edition,* is a systematically laid out one-of-a-kind All-in-one Gita-Dictionary, Gita-Grammar, Gita-Thesaurus, Gita-Reference and Gita-Index, in Devanagari Sanskrit-Hindi.

Sunita Narale

रत्नाकर-रचितम् गीतोपनिषद् (संस्कृत)

प्रो. रत्नाकर नराले,

9781897416723
Soft Cover

548

This Colour Coded Edition is world's first Sanskrit recension of the Gita, composed wholly in Anushtubh Shlokas. Its 1447 sholks are in side-by-side association with the 701 verses of the Bhagavad Gita.

गीता ज्ञान कोश (मराठी)

प्रो. रत्नाकर नराले,

978-1897416150
Soft Cover

480

May you be **a New learner, a Scholar, an Author, a Swami, a Professor or an Institution**, this is the right resource **for a critical study** for those who wish to go beyond.

RAMAYAN BOOKS

संगीत रामायण दोहावली

प्रो. रत्नाकर नराले,

978-1897416938
Soft Cover

630

इतिहास रचनेवाला संगीत महाकाव्य ऐसा न कभी हुआ न होगा. श्रीराम चंद्र व श्री हनुमान के सर्वतोपरी दैवी लीलाओं से भरा हुआ यह मनोरम व आध्यात्मिक गहनता से परिपूर्ण चरित्र जागतिक इतिहास में अनुपम हैं.

संगीत-श्रीकृष्ण-रामायण गीतमाला के गिने-चुने पुष्प

प्रो. रत्नाकर नराले,

978-1897416020
Soft Cover

130

संगीत-श्रीकृष्णायन तथा संगीत-श्रीरामायण के अंतर्गत गिने-चुने गानों का सुंदर संग्रह. संगीत सीखने एवं सिखाले के लिए मनोरंजक, स्फूर्तिदायक और भक्तिपूर्ण साधन.

DICTIONARY BOOKS

Flipped English Dictionary

प्रो. रत्नाकर नराले,

978-1897416624
Soft Cover

178

This valuable word search tool, is useful for Students, Teachers, Writers, Poets, Crossword Solvers, Special Education Professionals and Communication Disorder Specialists.

Sunita Narale

गीता का शब्दकोश और अनुक्रमणी

प्रो. रत्नाकर नराले,

978-1897416648
Soft Cover

445

Gita Ka Shabdakosh, New Edition, is a systematically laid out one-of-a-kind All-in-one Gita-Dictionary, Gita-Grammar, Gita-Thesaurus, Gita-Reference, Gita-Index and much more, in Devanagari Sanskrit-Hindi.

गीता पठनम्

प्रो. रत्नाकर नराले,

9781897416198
Soft Cover

70

Shlokas of the Bhagavad Gita are arranged in 8 syllable sections and two columns for proper singing and recitation. The text is printed in bigger size Devanagari Sanskrit Font for comfortable reading.

HISTORICAL BOOKS

भारतीय राष्ट्रीय आंदोलन और काशी की नागरीप्रचारिणी सभा
डा. राकेश कुमार दूबे
सह संपादक, पुस्तक भारती रिसर्च

978-1897416877
Soft Cover

320

काशी नागरीप्रचारिणी सभा के बहुआयामी कार्यों पर विस्तृत प्रकाश डाला गया है। सभा ने आम जनता द्वारा व्यवह्रत हिंदी भाषा और नागरी लिपि का प्रचार और उसी के माध्यम से संपूर्ण देश को एकसूत्र में बांधते का प्रयास किया।

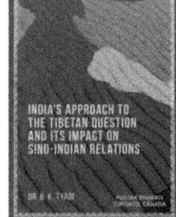

A Brief History of Trade Unionism in Mauritius

Rajpalsingh Allgoo
Mauritius

9781897416167
Soft Cover

270

History of Slavery and forced labour in Mauritius. How Mauritius was converted in to a colony. The British started a system called 'Indentured Labour.' An overview of the Trade Union movement in Mauritius from its beginning to the present day.

India's Approach to the Tibetan Question and its Impact on Sino-Indian Relations

Dr. BK Tyagi, India

978-1-897416-22-8
Soft Cover

206

It examines the two pronged question of India's dealings with her two important neighbours leading up to a politico-historical debate.

Dr. Ratnakar Narale

From India to Jamaica, Success story of a Pravasi

Dr. Ratnakar Narale[3]

I hope that as you read this, it will shed some enlightenment upon the challenges of our forefathers and how they bravely overcame them to rise up as successful citizens of their new country. It was my pleasure to put together the accounts and profiles and hope you find delight in reading it.

Henry Jaghai O. D., J. P.

The Early Indentured Workers

Sometimes divine coincidences (*Daivi Samyoga*) do occur. As the Editor-in-Chief of the Pustak Bharati Research Journal, Toronto, Canada, I am in the process of Editing and publishing our upcoming book "*Overseas Indians*" particularly focused on the old practice of voluntary agreement/indenture (*girmit*) to become a bonded labor, and with a wonderful divine coincidence the breathtaking book, "Journey from India to Jamaica," by Henry W. Jaghai, O.D., J.P. came to us for Editing and Publishing. Going through the awe-inspiring manuscript, and after fathoming the events of the life and achievements of Henry, it sinks in positively that, behind the astounding success of Henry, each relative of the greater Jaghai family, beginning with Arjun thorough Abrham, has played a role, direct or indirect, in this success story, beginning from an absolute scratch.

The book is a first hand narration of the chain of events and milestones by Jaghai's maternal grandmother Autaria of Bharatpur, about the saga that began with the travel of Arjun Jaghai of Rattapur (Uttar Pradesh, India) on March 16, 1911 from Calcutta on SS Indus for Jamaica. It is also a memorable account of achievements of this clan and how it contributed to the cultural, economic, educational, health, political, religious, social and sporting climate of Jamaica. Besides the overwhelming business success of Henry Jaghai, noteworthy are his passions and pastime in the sports activities of Horse breeding and Racing Championship, Cricket Matches and Team Captainship, Indo-Cultural contribution and International Travels

---

[3] Prof. Hindi, Ryerson University, Toronto, Canada

through Florida, Illinois, New York and Pennsylvania in USA; London, Italy, Switzerland, France, Austria, Belgium, Pakistan, Trinidad and Tobago, Guyana, Puerto Rico and India through Delhi, Jaipur, Calcutta, Bombay, Agra and Kashmir. This precious book, written by Henry to fulfill the old promise he made to his grandmother Autaria, is a collectors item for those readers who are interested in the history, achievements and contributions of the Indian Diaspora.

To this end, Stanley. A. Bajue, Ph. D. writes, I am more than pleased that Henry W. Jaghai, OD, JP, has asked me to write concerning the migration of *Indians* to *Jamaica*, and their experiences. I will briefly include a little of my own personal experience and thoughts on 'growing up Indian' in *Jamaica*.

When slavery ended in *Jamaica* in 1838, the sugar barons in there faced an immense shortage of labor, and the colonial masters, ever so concerned about the well being of their kindred folks abroad, turned to India and China for cheap labor. As pointed out by Mr. Jaghai in his book, '*Pardes,*' over 36, 000 Indians migrated to Jamaica as 'indentured servants.' The first migrants arrived in 1845 on the ship *Blondel* that embarked from *Calcutta* and landed at *Old Harbor Bay*. From there, the migrants were transported to various sugar estates in *Vere*. Migration continued until 1917.

The migrants were given 'five-year indentureship' contracts, and at the end of this period, they were afforded the opportunity to stay on the estates with incentives. Many accepted the offer and not quite a few were strong-armed in staying. Some returned to India, with repatriation in 1929 being the last one.

The migrants were segregated from others and were housed in 'barracks.' These barracks were mostly one-room row houses and thus migrants with families were crammed into each other. Monies for rent and other expenses were deducted from the meager wages of the migrants, and all reports indicated that health care and sanitary conditions were abominable. Water for drinking, cooking and other personal uses were likely obtained from polluted sources like rivers or gullies. Rainwater may have been an option for some.

The abominable living conditions and inhumane treatment of the migrants were unearthed and the Indian Raj, still under British jurisdiction, stopped the migration which officially ended in 1917. The 'Protector of Indians' in Jamaica may have had a hand in the matter.

As someone of Indian descent, I cannot help but feel the pain of my ancestors in this human tragedy. As someone put it, we have 'risen from the ashes.' But I must hasten to say that Indo-Jamaicans are not singular in this respect. So I still see my father and others toiling from dawn to dusk in the sugar cane fields of Vere, surviving mostly on 'dhal-bhat, roti and callaloo.' I am proud of the fact that Indian migrants and their descendants have made considerable contributions to the advancement of Jamaica, and the West

Indies in general, in spite of very many difficulties that were faced. Contributions have been made in the fields of agriculture, education, health care, sports, and politics, to mention a few areas. I cannot avoid mentioning *Dr. Winston Chutkan*, one of the very first Indo-Jamaican physician and a man of very humble background. Now there are very many such physicians and surgeons in Jamaica, including some from Guyana and Trinidad and Tobago.

The Indian culture has survived in Jamaica and has spread widely especially in the culinary field, as well as in music and dancing. 'Curried Goat and Rice, ' is a Jamaican favorite, especially on joyful occasions. 'Chicken Roti' is also a favorite of many, even in far-flung places like the USA and Canada. *Hindustani (Hindi)*, and *Urdu* the main language of the migrants, have all but died out in Jamaica. Other languages spoken by the migrants include *Bojpuri*, which is close to *Hindi*, and *Bengali*. *Urdu* is very close to *Hindi* as well but it is written in *Arabic* characters.

My maternal grandfather, who may have been a *Punjabi*, lived at Toll Gate with wife, Jane, and their children. His name is listed as *Alexander Mitchell* on my mother's birth certificate, so he must have worked on one of the many sugar estates in Vere owned by *Mitchell* as listed in Henry Jaghai's book '*Pardes.* ' But my grandfather was also called *Karkar Budhoo*, and *'Coolie' Jimmy*. The word *'Coolie'* is a derogatory term that is used in many places to refer to people of the Indian sub-continent. It is not unusual for some patients to refer to Indo-West Indian physicians and surgeons, and those from the *Indian* subcontinent as well, as '*coolie doctors.* '

We reaped enough rice to serve the family until next season. The rice seeds (dhan) were steamed overnight in a large 'kerosene' pan, sun dried on tarpaulins, beaten in a mortar, and then fanned to remove the chaff. Sometimes hulling was done using a foot operated 'dienkhi' owned by Sagar Williams at Gimme-me-bit in Vere. Later milling was done on a machine owned by Mr. Hayman at Kemps Hill. Split peas (matar dhal), hardi (yellow ginger), coriander, (dhanya), meeti, geera, lesun (garlic) and a few other ingredients were ground to a moist paste on a (grinding stone) and ready for the pot.

The Indian society is *maternal* in nature, so us boys of Indian origin did not help much with house hold chores. Some boys would help their parents with work on the estates during the holidays from school, but most of us spent our spare time playing cricket, fishing, or hunting birds with slingshots in the hunting season. We were hardly successful at bird hunting or fishing but there was more success at crab hunting. Crabs were plentiful during the rainy season in Vere, in May and again from August to October. Housework, a thankless job, was left to mothers and their daughters.

Most second and third generation Indo-Jamaican children excelled in elementary schools, but unfortunately, only a few went to high school (college) because of the associated expenses. There was only enough money to buy food, meet other expenses, and save to buy land and build a house of their own. So we owe much to our parents who sacrificed much in seeing us through the formative years and after. Much too is owed to many of our older siblings who stayed at home to care for the young ones while our parents toiled away in the cane fields. Moreover, many first generation Indo-Jamaican children served as translators for their Hindi or Urdu-speaking parents, so they were unable to attend school regularly. In addition, we have to thank former Chief Minister Norman Manley, who many years ago legalized Hindu and Muslim marriages. Prior to this the birth certificates of many of the children of Indo-Jamaicans show only the mother's name-the fathers name is missing. So these children had only one name- *Bajue, Mohan, Ramlal, Gobind, Budhoo, Bachue,* for example. Later on children were given two names-Stanley Bajue, Henry Jaghai, Roy Singh and so on.

This history needs to be told in much greater detail and taught in the schools as well. So I say 'well played Henry Jaghai.' I look forward to your third book on Indian migration to Jamaica.

And, thus in this course Henry Jaghai says, my paternal grandfather (Aaja), Jaghi, left his native country India in 1905 to work in Jamaica, which he always referred to as pardes (foreigh country). He and his wife Autaria (Aaji), became pardesi-jan, strangers in a new country, as did my maternal grandparents, Jaitun, Ragbar and Arjun. The stories they told me about the Motherland, the lifestyle they brought over and the culture and religion they practised, gave insight into the way of life in India. It was this strong cultural influence that impacted me most of all and created the fervour and passion in me to keep my grandparents' stories and cultural heritagealive.

To reconnect with my roots, I visited my ancestral home in 1987, which proved to be one of the most rewarding experiences of my life. With the help of Dr. Ajai Mansingh, his wife Laxmi Mansingh and Dr. Mansingh's brother, I was able to locate the village of Bahadurpur from which my paternal grandparents originated. While I was excited to trace back my roots, at the same time I was saddened at the state in which the people lived.

After this enlightening trip, Dr. Ajai Mansingh proposed writing a book together about the East Indians' journey to Jamaica as indentured labourers and what happened thereafter. In my role as researcher and financier, and the Mansingh's as authors, *Home Away from Home: 150 Years of Indian Presence in Jamaica,* was published in1999. Over the ensuing years, I became motivated to build up on *Home Away from Home,* fo cusing on the stories of pardesi-jan (strangers in a new country) and their descendants. *Pardes, Stories through the Eyes of a Pardesi's Grandson,* recaptures oral stories, cultural heritage and highlights of Indo-Jamaicans' accomplishments in Jamaica. After tracing the roots of my Nana in January of last year, through the help of Richard Francis and my friend, Ashutosh Diljun and his brother Avnindar Diljun and friend Lovey Dayal, I decided to write another book highlighting Arjun's story. This book and its contents were inspired by my origins as a poor boy who made a promise to my Aaji (grandmother) Autaria, to one day travel to her home village of Bahadurpur and help the villagers living in squalor.

Arjun's journey started one early morning in January, in the small village named Rattapur in India. Arjun was sent by his father Ori, to attend to his usual chores, of rounding up the cows, leading them to the milking shed and milking them to provide milk for the family, to start their day.

In the evenings, he would gather the cows from the pasture and lead them to their pen. Arjun had a faithful cow, who he affectionately named, "Baroda." He would tie her to the verandah post in the evenings, in preparation for the morning milking. On this unforgettable morning, Ori told Arjun to "go get the dude for breakfast," when Arjun went outside, his favorite cow Baroda was missing. Arjun began to panic and went in search of his cow. The search was in vain, Baroda was no where to be found. Frightened that his father would punish him, Arjun decided to stay away and did not return home. Hungry and tired, he eventually stopped to rest under a Neem tree, and started eating some of the berries from the tree. After a while a group of young people were passing by and saw Arjun eating the berries. In their conversation, Arjun learned that the British were recruiting workers to go abroad to work as Indentured laborers. His newly found friends were on their way to Faizabad, to sign up for the Indentureship program.

Arjun saw this as an opportunity to make a future for himself. He decided to take a risk, and went with his friends, on their journey to Faizabad. This journey, on foot took him through Milkipur, before arriving at this destination. On arrival, they were met by the British recruiters, who painted a glowing picture of life, as an Indentured laborer. This was very enticing to Arjun, who became very excited about his future. He made the decision to travel by train to Cawnpur to register as a labourer. The British Government provided temporary housing and food for all the recruits at the holding depot, until they reached the desired amount of workers they needed. Eventually, all the recruits were transported to Garden Reach, Calcutta, where the registration process was completed.

As part of the agreement they had to swear that they were going voluntarily and were asked questions that formed the terms of the five-year indentureship contract. Once they agreed to this stipulation their thumbprint was stamped on the form. On the historical day of March 20, 1911, Arjun along with his 812 shipmates (jahaji) departed the port of Calcutta on SS Indus in route to Jamaica West Indies.

On May 5, 1911 the SS Indus docked at the port in Kingston Jamaica. Arjun along with his shipmates, were assigned to work on Charles Gilpin Hudson's plantation and dairy farm, located on Marchpen road in Blairpen, Spanish Town St. Catherine. For the first five years Arjun worked very hard and was proficient at dairy farming job. Arjun worked with a similar breed of cows that he was accustomed to in India.

His days started out at 2 am. He would gather the milk containers and head toward the cow pen where he would milk the cow one by one in the stall. The milk truck would then travel to the condensery which was about a 10mile radius. By midmorning Arjun and his coworkers would take the cows out to the pasture and return to the dairy farm to clean up. By 4:30-5pm they would round up the cows and return them to the cow pen next to the milking stall. At the end of the first five-year indentureship, Arjun proved to be a very diligent worker who had impressed the busha. He was promoted to headman on the dairy farm. Arjun made the decision to sign up for a second five-year indentureship work.

As good as he was with his hands milking the cows; Arjun was even more skilful with his feet. He was an exceptional janghia dancer and had made sure to carry his colourful and patterned janghia pants from India. His combination of dancing skills and colourful costume always attracted attention and he soon formed a group called Arjun's Janghia Group.

After three years Arjun and his wife Jaitun moved to a leased property at 58 1/2 Spanish Town Road. In addition to living there, residents could plant crops and set up cottage industries. Some Indians specialized in barbering, carpentry, jewellery making, shoemaking, and tailoring. Kingston Pen soon became the headquarters for commercial, cultural and religious activities for the Pardes-jan and their descendants. While we lived in the area, I remember, the Caucasian Christian missionaries who travelled on bicycles who would visit us every Sunday. Under the big East Indian mango tree in the yard, they would hold Sunday school sessions to Christianize us, as they thought the religion of our Hindu parents was pagan.

After the indentureship period ended in 1917 and the last 5-year contract ended in 1922, the East Indians who decided to remain in Jamaica had a hard time sustaining themselves. To alleviate the situation the Governor Sir Arthur Richards, introduced The Government Relief Program (Bollo Work). The government employed ex-indentured Indians and their children to cultivate vegetable gardens on allotted lands. The produce from the fields would supply government institutions such as hospitals and prisons. Surplus crops were sold at the government retail station.

Workers on the farm were placed in groups and were supervised by a headman. My own father, Abraham Jaghai, Gam Bankasingh and James Purai worked as Bollo labourers. My grandfather Arjun and John Sankar were employed as headmen. They earned one pound and two shillings per week plus a free lunch daily.

In addition to vegetables, other crops were guinea grass, rice, sorghum and sweet corn. Water from underground was extracted to fill gadhas a process the Indians were accustomed to for irrigating their vegetable gardens.

In 1947, my grandparents bought a one-acre plot of land, in Simmons Pen at 66 1/2 Chisholm Avenue for one hundred and sixty pounds. This became our family home for years to come. My aunts, uncles and I grew up learning various trades and eventually started our own families creating a second generation of Indo-Jamaicans.

In 1951 Arjun and his family was faced with a natural disaster. It was a Friday night in August, Hurricane Charlie hit Jamaica resulting in devastation to the community and caused massive damages. His wattle and daub house was flattened by the hurricane. He and his family became homeless. They had to start all over again. He built a make shift temporary house from remnants of the storm.

In 1952, one of his prized milking cows, which he also named Baroda which unfortunately was fatally hit by a car. The driver demanded compensation for the damages done to his vehicle. Arjun had no choice but to sell two more of his milking cows to pay for the repairs. This misfortune forced his wife, Jaitun to seek employment to help with household expenses. Jaitun worked as a laborer in a vegetable garden which paid her three schillings per day. Both Arjun and Jaitun worked together totaling their earnings to pay the mortgage and provided food for the family. Arjun again sought employment as a headman at Ernest Ray Dairy Farm in Signam.

In October 1960, Arjun had a massive heart attack and he succumbed to his injuries and died at the age of 68 years old.

Emigration Pass for Jaghi, grandfather of Henry W. Jaghai, OD, JP, which authorized his departure from Calcutta to Jamaica, for the journey into indentureship, May 26, 1905

Emigration Pass for Autaria, grandmother of Henry W. Jaghai, OD, JP, which authorized her departure from Calcutta to Jamaica, for the journey into indentureship, May 26, 1905.

"Poverty was the greatest motivating factor in my life"
- *Jimmy Dean*

Henry Jaghai then tells us his long story in short. I was born on January 5, 1936, to parents Abraham Jaghai of Cherry Gardens and Ambrozine Arjun of 58 & 1/2 Spanish Town Road in Western Kingston. When the midwife delivered me, she told my mother that I was going to be called Money Man because of the size of my large ears. It is uncanny to think that her words have come true. Since then, I have often wondered if people really have the gift to predict the future.

At the tender age of six weeks old, my mother my paternal grandmother cared for me during the day while my mother ventured out to work. My mother worked tirelessly to give me the best life she could. My mother was finding life to be increasingly difficult with my father's absence from home, as he was not involved in my upbringing. In December 1940, at the age of four, my mother learned that my father was planning to give me away to the Alpha Orphanage. He'd decided to send me there, as it appeared I was now becoming a burden to my grandmother. Distressed to hear this news, she and my maternal grandfather, Nana Arjun, went to Police Station to report this. As the police approached the house, I saw them and ran to my grandmother to tell her, "Daata come with police for me." When they came into the yard, they found me barefoot, dressed in an oversized shirt that reached my ankles, and drinking strained water of boiled rice. I was surrounded by poverty and squalor. Though my grandmother cared deeply for me and did the best that she could with the resources she had, she was getting up in age, and was very frail and sickly. When she learned the group was there to take me back to live with my mother, she held on to me fiercely and declared she would not let me go. The police explained that I needed to attend school for my education very soon, and that my mother also missed me. So, I went to live with my mother once again.

In 1942, my grandmother died. while we attended the funeral, I can vividly remember someone lifting me up and passing me over her coffin three times. This was very heart-wrenching for me, as I was extremely close to her. Looking on, I recalled to memory that many a night, as a small child, she would reminisce about her life in India and the village she came from, Bahadurpur in Basti. She'd recount the many hardships she'd endured as well as the poverty that existed there. After listening to her many heartfelt stories, I made a promise to my grandmother that I would visit her village in India and help the children there. With the help of God I was able to fulfill my promise by awarding scholarships annually to the poor children, provided bedding supplies to the elderly, and built a temple in her and honor which is erected in her village.

I had always had an interest in law but unfortunately I could not pursue this dream due to poverty. Instead I decided to learn a trade in auto mechanics. This career path was due in large part to my grandfather Arjun, who encouraged me to become an apprentice mechanic at Houranay'sGarage. While working at the garage, I had to take the public bus service to go back and forth from work. I was often ridiculed by the passengers on the bus who would heckle me because of my dirty appearance from working with oil and grease during the day. I would often be told to go to the back of the bus. To avoid the shame and scorn I experienced during those trips, I decided to purchase a bicycle and told my mother of my plans. She said she would help me if I got some of the money, so I inquired about working next door at the Zaidie Tobacco Shop, on my lunch break. I got the job there sharpening the knives they used to cut the tobacco. I was able to earn extra money towards the purchase of my bicycle.

I continued working at the garage, earning two shillings a week. At the end of one year I decided to ask my employer if he would be willing to pay me a little bit more, as I was now more advanced in my craft. He promptly turned me out of his establishment, saying "don't come back!" I was now out of a job. "This was pure sufferation." Without a job, I had no other recourse but to hustle to make some money. I would go to my relatives' home in Barbican, and pick fruits such as mangoes and ackee. I would then peddle my produce to a local vendor who would in turn sell them to customers on the street side. This was how I was able to earn some money to help out the family at home.

In 1953, a spark of luck hit me when I met an Indian gentleman by the name of Herbert Maragh. He was able to secure a job for me at John Crook Limited. There I earned 15 shillings per week.Now I was able to start saving one pound per week at the Government Savings Bank on Tower Street. I was also able to save money by going to my mother's kitchen at lunchtime to get free lunch. After leaving work at 5pm, I would continue to do odd jobs to earn extra money. I also worked privately fixing cars which further contributed to my savings. On one occasion, I recall that I had gotten a car to work on. When the work was complete, some friends and I decided to take it for a drive. On our trip back, I was at the wheel as we were going around the car suddenly flipped over. I sustained a fractured arm in the accident, and this marked the beginning of another streak of bad luck for me. With the hand still injured, I couldn't perform adequately, so I was soon terminated. From the end of 1953, I was out of a job, until 1966, when Herbert Maragh, for the second time, got me a job at Motor Sales as a full fledged mechanic. I was there for 11 years.

My affiliation with St. Thomas Aquinas as an altar server of the church paved the way for a significant milestone in my life. It was there that I laid eyes on a church attendee, the fair maiden, Myrtle Hill Suckie of Whitehall Avenue, and was smitten by her beauty. I, at the young age of 18, asked Myrtle, at the tender age of 17, to marry me. We were wed on April 25, 1954.

BUSINESS SUCCESS

I was determined that my children would have an easier life than I did. In 1968, I worked hard and diligently and finally was able to establish my own garage and auto parts business, Jaghai's Garage Ltd. Initially, the company dealt exclusively with the sale of new and used auto parts for British made cars but as the global market changed, I extended the business operations to the sale of Japanese auto parts. The company, which over time engaged the services of all of my sons, flourished to become the leading auto parts dealer between 1970 and early 1990.

PASTIMES

With the business successfully established, I could finally afford to spend time on a hobby I loved, cricket. I had started playing schoolboy cricket when I was ten years old. This passion has remained with me throughout my life. In 1954, I formed the All Indian Cricket Team, assuming the roles of financier, manager and captain for a few years. The team competed in many local competitions and won several trophies - the most prestigious being the Rankin Cup.

In 1973, accompanied by a large contingent of family and friends as supporters, the team toured Trinidad and Guyana, where we won most of our matches. It was a good occasion where sporting, cultural and social activities merged to make the tour an unforgettable experience.

During my 1973 Trinidad and Guyana cricket tour with the Balraam Championship team, I met Dr CheddieJaggan, President of Guyana. Dr Jaggan and Dr Balwant Singh were particularly helpful in accommodating the team at the Ghandi Youth Organisation Center in Georgeton, Guyana.

PIGEON RACING CHAMPIONSHIP

Another hobby of mine was horse racing. I joined the Horse Club in the 1960's and remained an active member until it became defunct in the 1970's due to the mass migration of many of its members.

I had over 300 pigeons, which I bred and raced. In the 1960's, my pigeon, Chantilly, clocked the fastest time of 58 minutes, flying from Mandeville to Rosalie Avenue, Kingston, a record which to date has not been broken. In 1999, I, along with other pigeon racing enthusiasts decided to form a new club, which we named Jamaica Pigeon Racing Club (JRPC). Meetings were held at my Bombay Stud Farm. In 2000, the Jamaica Pigeon Racing Club was revived and I served as its president for that year. I contributed financially towards the purchase of the racing clocks for the club and assisted members with the transportation for the training of the birds.

I made my office on the farm available for meetings and special occasions during the life of the JRPC. I competed in several races spanning the length and breadth of Jamaica. In 2009, I entered and won most of the races organized by the club and was awarded the Champion Loft Trophy for the year. The Staff Van Reet and Black Diamond strains of horse were helpful in my winning the championship.

HORSE RACING

My other notable interest is my love for horses. I acquired my first horse farm on 25 acres in Spring Gardens, St. Catherine known as Rockmore Farm from trainer Ren Gonsalves in 1968. I already boarded Latchmie Ranee, Dainty Petal and Tuneful Goddess there. When I purchased the farm, I bought it with the stallion Jobber Bill along with two mares, Sheila and Scapper Floor. I then bought True Lover, Shenandoah and NRA as mares. I also bought Chantilly, My Love and Funny Cut from Orange Valley Estates. The terrain was very hilly and not suitable for horses.

My objective at this time was to breed horses to race myself. In 1972, I received permission from Bob Mayall as manager of the racetrack to build a 17-stall barn, and office on the compound. In 1976, I then purchased the former Supreme Farm at Bushy Park, St. Catherine. The farm was on 14 acres of land. I acquired a further adjoining 6 acres, making it 20 acres in total. I named the farm Bombay Stud Farm. At the farm, I had A class mares; Polka Dotty, Glory's Mariposa, Chan Chan, Miss America, Paddy's Doll, Late Moon, Story Time, and Wrong Reason. Close Call was the first stallion that stood at the farm. I then imported Big Prince to stand as a stallion, as well as local top-class racer Reca. Reca won the Jamaica Derby, Governor's Cup, and the Gold Cup. I subsequently purchased him and won four races with him including the Guiness Mile and Mark Twain Trophy. At this farm, we produced 1989 Guineas winner Lady Geeta, 1980 Governor's Cup winner Shady Grove, along with A class winners Tulsie Kumar, Lashanda's Devil and Lady Vasanti. Other useful performers were Lady Maharanee, Sir Henry Kumar and many others. At Bushy Park we held many Indian functions filled with good memories.

In 1990, I transitioned from being a hobby breeder to a commercial breeder by procuring the Family Farm in Grange, St. Catherine on 111 acres. I had already sent six mares to be covered by the stallion Restless Thief, and boarded them there. Bobby Clarke notified me that the farm was to be sold, which led to me acquiring it. I also purchased most of the stock there, including the two stallions, Restless Thief and Joe Slew, and about fifteen mares including Music Belle, Glen Afric, Nicolina, Sky Train, and Babydun. I brought Big Prince along with the remaining mares from Bushy Park. I purchased many other mares both locally and imported from the United States. I imported Sir Lal Bahadur as a stallion followed by Holy Runner,

At this farm we produced 2007 Superstakes winner, Major Mayer and 2008 Triple Crown winner Alsafra, who won the Derby, St. Leger, 1000 Guineas and also the Oaks. Other classic winners were Lady Bangalore (1998 Oaks), Latonia (2004 1000 Guineas and Oaks), Run Papa Run (2004 St. Leger), Rum Talk (2007 2000 Guineas and St. Leger), Al Fouzia (2010 1000 Guineas), Niphal (2011 1000 Guineas), Big Man Boyu (2011 2000 Guineas), Lady Abhijita (2013 Oaks), and I Am Di One (2019 1000 Guineas). Governor's Cup winners were Run Papa Run in 2004, and It Is I in 2008. We also had success in Trinidad, breeding Flying Millie a multiple Grade-1 winner, and Legally Ready 2011 W.I. Bred 2yo Fillies Championship winner. We also raced Sir Rajah Raeby, Lady Bangalore, Sir Mohandas Baba, Sir GobinHarrilal, Lady Baroda and Lady Jaipur in Trinidad. My trainers in Trinidad were Desmond Sagar and Neal Maharaj, and my agent was Rolf Bartolo.

I won the Champion Breeder Award 10 years. Of these 10 years, 8 were consecutive from 1997 to 2004, and then again in 2007 and 2008. In 1999, I won the most ever races as a breeder with 105 wins. In 1997, I received the None Such Award and in 2004 was inducted into the Jamaica Racing Hall of Fame. For the first 50 years of horse racing at Caymanas Park, I was the All Time Leading Breeder by stakes earned. As a breeder, I have won over 1500 races.

The names I have given my fillies are Lady Abhijita, Lady Agra, Lady Ajiban, Lady Aleema, Lady Anandi, Lady Anarkali, Lady Arti, Lady Atwaree, Lady Bahin, Lady Bakul, Lady Ballari, Lady Bangadesh, Lady Bangalie, Lady Bangalore, Lady Bansari, Lady Baroda, Lady Basti, Lady Basanti, Lady Bastipur, Lady Chachi, Lady Chameli, Lady Chandra, Lady Chandrika, Lady Chatura, Lady Chiriya, Lady Danragie, Lady Devi, Lady Diwali, Lady Dularie, Lady Faizabad, Lady Gangadeo, Lady Gauri, Lady Geeta, Lady Geetadeo, Lady Gorakhpur, Lady Hyderabad, Lady Indira, Lady Jaanwar, Lady Jagranee, Lady Jagrati, Lady Jaipur, Lady Jameela, Lady Jamuna, Lady Jayshree, Lady Kaloutie, Lady Kamla, Lady Kampoor, Lady Kanchan, Lady Kumari, Lady Lachmin, Lady Latika, Lady Madras, Lady Maharanee, Lady Mala, Lady Maragin, Lady Nagara, Lady Nagin, Lady Najariya, Lady Najeeban, Lady Nanda, Lady Noorie, Lady Pakeezah, Lady Parbattie, Lady Phagwah, Lady Pooja, Lady Punjab, Lady Punjabi, Lady Radha, Lady Rajkumari, Lady Rakwalaay, Lady Ramkali, Lady Ramragie, Lady Rattapur, Lady Rukmini, Lady Rupamani, Lady Sabita, Lady Saburi, Lady Sapna, Lady Sattie, **Lady Seeta** *(picture bellow is for example, all pictures are in the book)*, Lady Seetadeo, Lady Shabani, Lady Shalimar, Lady Shakeera, Lady Shanti, Lady Shareeda, Lady Sharmeela, Lady Sharvani, Lady Silsila, Lady Suhaagraat, Lady Suneeta, Lady Suraanee, Lady Suragie, Lady Tarkari, Lady Tulasi, Lady Vasanti, Lady Janakpur, Lady Pujarie, Lady

Gobindia, Lady Sarsutta and Lady Seetarani. The colts are Tulsie Kumar, Sikhandar, Sir Abbas Mangal, Sir Ananda Baba, Sir Arjun Babu, Sir Badri Bansilal, Sir Banbihari, Sir Bhola Baba, Sir Chacha Baba, Sir Ganesh Baba, Sir Ganga Kumar, Sir GobinHarrilal, Sir Henry Kumar, Sir Jaadu Baba, Sir Jhunjhun Wala, Sir KedarRamlal, Sir Kishore Kumar, Sir Kisson Lal, Sir Krishna Baba, Sir Kunjabihari, Sir Mohandas Baba, Sir Mohan Gopal, Sir Muni Brijmohan, Sir Pardasie Baba, Sir Raja Kumar, Sir Rajah Raeby, Sir Rajesh Pattasar, Sir Rama Tulsidas, Sir Ramjas Jagdeo, Sir RamjasRamlal, Sir Ramnath Gupta, Sir Ravi Sankur, Sir Rohan Baba, Sir Rohanlal Baba, Sir Rohan Tulsidas, Sir Sadhu Baba, Sir Sastri Bahadur, Sir Shankar Dada, Sir Thakur Baba, Sir Vishnu Kumar, Sir Jagat Baba, Sir Ram Sundar, Sir JeewanBabula, Sir Lal Beharie, Sir Ram Hari, Sir Jahaji Bhai, Sir Hajarie Baba, Sir RagbarBapi, Sir Ganga Jamuna, Sir Anil Tilakram, Sir Sunil Bhaijee and Sir Chowtie Lal.

Lady Seeta

1997 "NONE SUCH AWARD"

Mr. Danny Melville (L) presents the 1997 None Such Award to Mr. Henry W. Jaghai O.D.J.P. Owner/Breeder of Bombay Stud Farm

Excellence in horseracing plaque awarded to Henry Jaghai OD., JP, on September 2019. He won the Breeder's Championship for 10 years

Dr. Ratnakar Narale

LOVE FOR CRICKET

I loved-cricket. I had started playing school boy cricket when I was ten years old. This passion has remained with me throughout my life. In 1954, I formed the All Indian Cricket Team, assuming the roles of financier, manager and captain for a few years. The team competed in many local competitions and won several trophies-the most prestigious being the Rankin C up.

Group photograph of 1973 all Indian Balraam Cup Champion cricket team, which toured Trinidad and Guyana. Henry W. Jaghai was team manager and player.Standing (L-R): Carlton Lawla, William Mitchell, Henry W. Jaghai, Maurice Rambana, Kenneth Beepat, and KeithSingh. Sitting (L-R): Robert Maragh, Adolphus Arjun, Danny Lewis–Captain, Lynval Rhyman, Aston Rhyman, and AliBahadur. Pictures of all teams are in the book.

In 1944, the All Indian Cricket Club won the Hamilton Cup. The team consisted of Capt. Bertie Smith, Vice-captain Munesar, Baby Latchman, George Pagu, John Barker, C. Jullur, Wilfred Dean, Charles Harry, Solomon Lal, Baggabaga Maragh, and CecilAllan.

In 1949, the All Indian Recreation cricket team entered the Junior Cup competi- tion. The team consisted of Austin Jadusingh, CaltapJadusingh, Willie Budhoo, Mannie Budhoo, Daniel Mykoo, Solomon Lal, Fredrick Lal, Luluman Maragh, Samuel Harry, Arnold Abdully, Ernest Bulli, Adolphus Lal, and David Ramdeen.

In 1952, Arthur Sardarsingh entered the Carib Cup competition with most of the players from the 1949 team along with two additional players, Joe Maragh and Robert Maragh. This team was successful and emerged winners of the Carib Cup. Most of the players from this team eventually migrated to England.

In 1953, Samuel Singh formed the Indian Youth Cricket Team with many young players. This cricket club started at the home of Singh at 167 Spanish Town Road, St Andrew. The club secretary was Ralph "Littleman" Binda and members of this new club were Aston Arjun, Adolphus Arjun, Henry W. Jaghai, Oscar Singh, Bal- am Hardiall, StaggyHardiall, Moses Watson, Ruffus Ramsay, Hugh Roy Damalie, David Ramdeen, Cecil Barker, Jack Thompson, Finger Thompson, Melvin Dama- lie, and Sucksingh Badrambally. This group of players played many curry goat and friendly matches.

In 1955 and 1958, this group of players entered the Hamilton Cup competition.
Other players that joined the team were Dudus Williams, Harry Maragh, Sydney Maragh, Alvin Maragh, Baby Rhyman, Aston Rhyman, Raymond Mahabir, Leonard Chambers, Keith Singh, Colin Hinds, Donald Maragh, Alfred Bahadur, JoeMaragh, Robert Maragh, Roy Banasee, and Morris Rambana.

In 1959-1960 Munesar Maragh became manager for the All Indian Cricket Team. Regular meetings were held at his home at Spanish Town Road in St Andrew. The All Indian team entered the Rankin Cup competition in 1960. Before match- eswere played, the team members would gather at the manager's home and he would conduct puja prayers before each game. The team was successful and won the Rankin Cupthat year.

Again, in 1960, the team entered the Masterton cricket competition, under the leadership of Captain Rama Maragh and won. That year the team had two back-to-back wins. After 1960, members of the team went to play for different teams, resulting in a fragmentation of the team.

In 1965, I decided to put another all-Indian cricket team together and entered the Masterton Cup cricket competition.

In 1968, I became manager and captain of a new team, Jaghai Garage Cricket Team and entered in the Rankin Cup cricket competi- tion.
In 1969, Balraam Maragh donated a trophy, the Balraam Trophy for Indian players. In 1970, the winners of the first Balraam Trophy went to Indian Youth Cricket Club, Manager Arjun Bhalai, and Captain Glen Harry. In 1973 the All Indian Junior Cricket Team won the competition. In 1983 there was another all-Indian cricket club, under my management. In 1985, the All Indian Cricket Club entered and won the Gleaner K.O Championship.

INDO-CULTURAL CONTRIBUTION
My Aaji, Nani and Nana inspired me so much with their culture that it became an integral

part of my life. To this day, I still eat my roti and dhal, listen to my Indian music and attend cultural get togethers to hear the musicians play and watch the dancers move rhythmically in their colourful costumes.

My passion for the preservation and propagation of the Indian culture in Jamaica has been far-reaching and very tangibly demonstrated. I was instrumental in giving and getting financial support to build Jamaica's first ever Hindu temple – The Sanatan Dharma Mandir in 1976. In 1984, I donated my premises at 10 Henderson Avenue to the Prema Sastsangh to house its temple as well as its medical clinic. In 1978 I, along with other East Indians formed The Indo-Jamaican Cultural Society, which was committed to the promotion, propagation and preservation of East Indian culture in Jamaica. The society was instrumental in organizing the 150th celebration and re-enactment of the landing of the first set of East Indians in Jamaica. 9Between 1978 and 1990, I hosted the grand Phagwah and Diwali festivals on my premises, at Bombay Stud Farm in Bushy Park, St. Catherine. I promoted numerous stage shows featuring Indian dancers, musicians, and singers from Jamaica, Trinidad and Guyana. In the early 1990's, I spearheaded two cultural tours hosted in Trinidad, and sponsored by UNESCO.

My fervour for the Hindu culture led me to produce eight LPs of traditional Indian folk music of the Caribbean, utilizing local talents as well as performers from Canada, Guyana, India, Trinidad, and the United Kingdom. In my ongoing quest to preserve the culture of my forefathers, I decided to record all information in print - a medium that could be passed down to future generations. I commissioned the services of researchers to write a book starting with the historical journey of the East Indian indentured labourers and how they integrated to become part of the cultural, economic, political, and social fabric of Jamaica. The book, Home Away from Home: 150 Years of IndianPresencein Jamaica, was launched in 1999.

On Monday, October 15, 2007, I was invested by the Jamaican Government with the insignia of the Order of Distinction for my contribution to the development of East Indian culture in Jamaica.

Despite having retired and now living in Florida, I still try to promote the culture as much as I can. I am readily available to give information to enquiring minds and to share my many resources (cultural books and music records) with others in the Indo-Caribbean Diaspora. I was recognized by Jayadevi Arts Inc., an organization committed to the rejuvenation of Indo-Caribbean cultural and artistic life in the United States. I received an award from them on Saturday, January 25, 2014 at the Walter C. Young Performing Arts Centre, Pembroke Pines, Florida for my contribution to Indo-Caribbean culture.

In the 1980's, I produced eight volumes of "Indian Folk Songs of the Caribbean." I commissioned Ramlal Malgie to write three songs of the journey from India to Jamaica. The first of which was "PalisadoesOhrniJahaaj, " the second was "Jamaica Pardesi

Chale" performed by Berverly Pancham, and the third was "Blundell Toe Peheli Jahaaj" performed by Petronia Dean.

EXEMPLARY COMMUNITY SERVICE

As a Justice of the Peace for twenty-five years, I was awarded the prestigious Golden Scale Award in 2002 by the Lay Magistrates Association for being the most outstanding Justice of the Peace in the county of Surrey.

PARDES BOOK LAUNCH

In 2015, I released Pardes: Stories Through The Eyes of a Pardesi's Grandson inspired by my grandparents Jaghi and Autaria. The publication featured the stories of the journey made by my grandparents and other East Indian indentured immigrants to Jamaica and the subsequent achievements of their descendants. It also depicts the cultural and religious influences they brought to Jamaica. In September 2015, I held a launch for the book, in Miramar, Florida to celebrate and promote its release. The launch was well attended, and the program consisted of Indian cultural performances. Many of those featured in the book were present.

Pardes book launch at St. Bartholomew Hall, Miramar, Florida

Overseas Literature of Indian Diaspora

Dr. P.K. Pandia[4]

Abstract:
Literature essentially reflects the way of life and that is what defines literature. It is aptly said that literature mirrors the society and the Indian diasporic writers' literature also mirrors the society of the country in which they are living and where they or their forefathers have lived earlier. In a way, the literature is the narration of the experiences or the fancy a writer may have in the course of his/ her life. It is but very natural for the overseas writers of Indian Diaspora to express their literary creativity on such experiences and themes. Indian Diasporic writers are emotionally attached to their indigenous country to a great extent. Their literature acquaints the world with the kind of Indians they are. It is thanks to the Indian Diaspora that the world is psychologically prepared to interact with Indians according to their belief system. This happens only when fellow Indians, who are settled abroad, help India in spreading Indian culture and traditions to all the corners in the world through their literature. The fact is that the Indian Diasporic writers belong to such a category of the writers which keeps the spirit of India alive outside India too.

The Indian Diaspora is a generic term to identify the people who migrated from territories that are well within the borders of the Republic of India. It is used for their forefthers, as well. The Indian Diaspora is available practically almost in every part of the world. There are more than a million Indians each in eleven countries. Twenty-two countries have got at least a hundred thousand ethnic Indians. Broadly speaking, there are three categories of overseas Indians.

• **NRI**s stay abroad for indefinite period for whatever purpose and a sizable number live in the Gulf countries.

• **PIO**s are such overseas Indians who have become the citizen of the countries of their settlement.

---

[4] Dr. P.K. Pandia, Educationist, Churu, Rajasthan

- **Stateless Persons of Indian Origin (SPIO)** are such persons who do not have documents to substantiate their Indian Origin and a good number of them live in Myanmar and Sri Lanka.

The powerful Indian Diaspora plays an important role in safeguarding and promoting India's interest abroad. It plays the role of ambassadors abroad. This is more so in the fields of literature, arts, economic development, ICT, medical science, culture, education, etc.

The role of literature in the Indian Diaspora needs to be further highlighted. The Diaspora's literary achievements have not just increased India's image in the world but have also highlighted their personal image, internationally. The literary contribution of these writers has also established a direct and mutually-reinforcing synergy between India and the international community. It is very important to mention here the overseas literary works of the Indian Diaspora such as Jhumpa Lahiri, Kovid Gupta, V. S. Naipaul, Kiran Desai, Agha Shahid Ali, Rohinton Mistry and Salman Rushdie, who are of Indian descent. Their literary output comes in the broader category of post-colonial literature. The literature from previously colonized countries here refers to India.

The overseas literature is a comparatively recent development, being only one and a half centuries old or so. Travels of Dean Mahomet, a travel narrative by Sake Dean Mahomet is known as the first book by an Indian in English that was brought out in England in 1793. In the initial stage, the overseas literature was greatly influenced by the Western literature. In the beginning Indian Diasporic writers would use such English that was pure for an Englishman to convey an experience which was essentially an Indian. It is appropriate to mention that Dhan Gopal Mukerji (1890–1936) has the privilege of being the first Indian author to win a literary award in the United States. Lakshmi Holmström has remarked about the trend in the following words, "The writers of the 1930s were fortunate because after many years of use, English had become an Indian language used widely and at different levels of society, and therefore they could experiment more boldly and from a more secure position."

V. S. Naipaul who is a third generation Indian from Trinidad and Tobago has the privilege of being a Nobel Prize laureate. In his works Naipaul expresses the ideas of homeland, rootlessness and his own personal feelings towards India.

Nirad C. Chaudhuri (1897–1999), a non-fiction writer, has earned popularity for his The Autobiography of an Unknown Indian (1951). He has narrated his life experiences and influences in the autobiography. The book established him one of India's greatest writers. It was published in 1951. The autobiography describes the life of the writer from the time he was born in 1897 in Bangladesh to his youth in Calcutta. The book beautifully captures every minute detail of his surroundings and of modern India. It has won him the global acclaim. Even the legendary Winston Churchill considered it one of the best books he had ever read. It has been included as one of the few Indian contributions in The New Oxford Book of English Prose, as well

Vikram Seth has brought out The Golden Gate (1986) and A Suitable Boy (1994). Vikram Seth's A Suitable Boy was published in 1993. This is one of the longest novels ever published in a single volume in English. The novel in which a family is looking for a suitable boy to marry the daughter is based on the theme of India post-partition. As a writer he has made use of a purer English and more realistic themes. His focus as a fan of Jane Austen is on the story, its details and its twists and turns. Vikram Seth is known far and wide both as a novelist and poet. But regrettably his remarkable achievement as a versatile and prolific poet has mostly gone unrecognized.

Mulk Raj Anand published The Private Life of an Indian Prince in 1953. This book is considered as one of Anand's masterpieces. The story is based on the theme of abolition of princely states in India while focusing on the life of a King and his fascination towards one of his mistresses. The story has blended some real life incidents which are beautifully woven into fiction.

Amitav Ghosh who is the author of The Circle of Reason has contributed immensely to the overseas literature. It was his debut novel in 1986. The Shadow Lines (1988), The Calcutta Chromosome (1995), The Glass Palace (2000), The Hungry Tide (2004), and Sea of Poppies (2008), the first volume of The Ibis trilogy, set in the 1830s, just before the Opium War, which captures the colonial history of the East are his major works. His latest work River of Smoke (2011) and his second volume of The Ibis trilogy are also very famous. The_Glass_Palace by Amitav Ghosh has won the Grand Prize for Fiction at the Frankfurt International e-Book Awards in 2001. The story is set in Burma. It highlights various issues related to the British invasion in 1885. The novel beautifully delineates the circumstances and incidents that made Burma, India and Malaya what they are today. This story of the empire, love, the changing society etc is very absorbing.

Jhumpa Lahiri's The Interpreter of Maladies which was published in 1999 and won the Pulitzer Prize for Fiction and the Hemingway Foundation/PEN Award in the year 2000 is a collection of nine stories. The stories portray the lives of Indians and Indian Americans who are sandwiched between the two cultures.

Rohinton Mistry is an India born Canadian author who has got a Neustadt International Prize for Literature laureate in 2012. Tales from Firozsha Baag (1987) was his debut book. It is a collection of 11 short stories. Rohinton Mistry's A Fine Balance is the second novel which was published in 1995. Just like his first novel, Such A Long Journey, this novel too elicited good response from the readers across the globe. The second novel moves around various characters in Mumbai. The story based on friendship and love runs in the book which keeps the readers glued to the novel till the end.

Dr. P.K. Pandia

Kiran Desai has written The Inheritance of Loss. The book was written over a period of seven years after her debut book. It brings out different conflicts between various Indian groups, in the past and at present. It highlights the fact in what way people find the English lifestyle fascinating. The book also captures the perception of various opportunities in the US. The book won Desai the Man Booker Prize in 2006 and the National Book Critics Circle Fiction Award among other awards.

One of the most known writers among the post colonial writers is Salman Rushdie who was born in India. At present he is living in America. Rushdie became very famous with his work Midnight's Children. Midnight's Children has described the journey of India from British rule to independence and then partition. The book got a great response, winning the Booker Prize in 1981 and the "Booker of Bookers" Prize twice – in 1993 and 2008! The book has reached various parts of the country including Kashmir, Agra and Mumbai, incorporating many real historic events. The book has got the coveted place in the List of 100 Best Novels of all time. This book has set a new trend of writing. He has made use of a hybrid language in his work. His English is full of Indian terms to convey a theme that could be viewed as representing the vast canvas of India. Salman Rushdie is generally classified under the magic realism mode of writing most popularly associated with Gabriel García Márquez.

Vikram Chandra is also a popular author. He moves a lot between India and the United States. He has earned critical acclaim for writing Red Earth and Pouring Rain. It won the 1996 Commonwealth Writers' Prize for Best First Book. The novel was inspired by the biography of James Skinner who was a legendary nineteenth-century Anglo-Indian soldier. It also weaves Indian myths and history into a story of three college kids. The book describes the tale of two characters. It has got a mythological touch with a modern subplot

Suketu Mehta is a New York based writer. He was born in India and was raised in Mumbai in his early years. He described his experiences in Mumbai in his great work Maximum City. His book was published in 2004. He was a Pulitzer Prize finalist in 2005. The book is a blend of travel writing, a journal, a socio-political analysis of people and wonders of Mumbai. It won the 2005 Vodafone Crossword Book Award. The Economist named Maximum City as one of its books of the year for 2004. The book was also shortlisted for the 2005 Samuel Johnson Prize.

Arvind Adiga has received the Man Booker Prize for his debut novel The White Tiger in 2008.

Davidar has set his The House of Blue Mangoes in Southern Tamil Nadu. In both of his books, he has blended geography and politics with the narrative. Shreekumar Varma has narrated the unique matriarchal system and the sammandham system of marriage in his novel Lament of Mohini (2000), while writing about the Namboodiris and the aristocrats of Kerala.

Among some prominent modern expatriate Indian poets who write in English are: Agha Shahid Ali, Sujata Bhatt, Richard Crasta, Yuyutsu Sharma, Tabish Khair, Vikram Seth etc. Some bilingual writers such as Paigham Afaqui with his novel Makaan in 1989 have also made remarkable contributions.

The overseas literature has its own share of controversy as well. When Rushdie remarked in his book – "the ironic proposition that India's best writing since independence may have been done in the language of the departed imperialists" is simply too much for some authors to digest. This created a lot of resentment among many writers. In his book, Amit Chaudhuri has countered remarking, "Can it be true that Indian writing, that endlessly rich, complex and problematic entity, is to be represented by a handful of writers who write in English, who live in England or America and whom one might have met at a party?"

Conclusion

The Indian diaspora has immensely contributed in the field of literature. Some of the Indian Diasporic writers are globally known. This adds feathers to the cap of India as well. The standard of the Indian Diasporic literature has, over the period of time, reached the global standard and the portrayal of India merits the attention of the global community towards India. The literary style and the subject matter of the literature by the Indian Diaspora have changed and are changing constantly according to the need of hour. Due to extraordinary diversity and geographical spread the genre, the language, the treatment, literary devices and the writing style are changing, depending upon each segment of Diaspora. A significant segment of Indian Diaspora lives in the Gulf countries. The approach towards the Indian Diaspora in the Gulf is primarily welfare oriented and remittance centric as there are mainly workers. As such their literary outcome is not significant. But the overseas literature by the Diaspora in the developed world is multifaceted. Here it aims at making India a knowledge power. The ICT and transportation revolution and the global access of media are bringing about a major change in the nature of literature between the Diasporas and their country of origin. There is still a need for vibrant interaction among the overseas Indians and India. The Indian Council for Cultural Relations should play a bigger role to strengthen ties in this direction. It is a good sign that the overseas literature written by Indian Diaspora is well received by the international community.

References

1. Singh, Bijender. "Indian Writing in English: Critical Insights." New Delhi, Authorspress, 2014.
2. Mehrotra, Arvind Krishna (ed.). A History of Indian Literature in English. New York: Columbia University Press, 2003. Distributed by Doaba Books Shanti Mohan House 16, Ansari Road, New Delhi.
3. Haq, Rubana (ed.). The Golden Treasury of Writers Workshop Poetry. Kolkata: Writers Workshop,

2008.
4. Hoskote, Ranjit (ed.). Reasons for Belonging: Fourteen Contemporary Indian Poets. Viking/Penguin Books India, New Delhi, 2002.
5. Mehrotra, Arvind Krishna (ed.). The Oxford India Anthology of Twelve Modern Indian Poets. Calcutta: Oxford University Press, 1992.
6. Prem, PCK. English Poetry in India: A Comprehensive Survey of Trends and Thought Patterns New Delhi: Authorspress, 2011.ASIN 8172736029
7. Sadana, Rashmi. "Writing in English," in The Cambridge Companion to Modern Indian Culture. Cambridge: Cambridge University Press, 2012.
8. Indian Writing in English | Men and Dreams in the Dhauladhar by Novels by Indian Authors - Kochery C Shibu
9. Haq, Kaiser (ed.). Contemporary Indian Poetry. Columbus: Ohio State University Press, 1990.
10. Joseph, Margaret Paul. "Jasmine on a String: a Survey of Women Writing English Fiction in India." Oxford University Press, 2014.
11. King, Bruce Alvin. Modern Indian Poetry in English: Revised Edition. New Delhi: Oxford University Press, 1987, rev. 2001.
12. King, Bruce Alvin. Three Indian Poets: Nissim Ezekiel, A K Ramanujan, Dom Moraes. Madras: Oxford University Press, 1991.
13. Parthasarathy, R. (ed.). Ten Twentieth-Century Indian Poets (New Poetry in India). New Delhi: Oxford University Press, 1976.
14. Reddy, T. Vasudeva. A Critical Survey of Indo-English Poetry New Delhi: Authorspress, 2016.ASIN 9352072499
15. Roy, Pinaki. "Encountering the West: A Very Brief Overview of the Indian Diasporic Novelists". Journal of Higher Education and Research Society (ISSN 2321-9432) 1(1).
16. Roy, Pinaki. "Dramatic Chronicle: A Very Brief Review of the Growth of Indian English Plays". Indian Drama in English: Some Perspectives. Ed. Kaushik, A.S. New Delhi: Atlantic Publishers and Distributors Pvt. Ltd., 2013 (ISBN 978-81-269-1772-3). pp. 272–87.
17. Sadana, Rashmi. English Heart, Hindi Heartland: the Political Life of Literature in India. Berkeley: University of California Press, 2012.
18. Srikanth, Rajini. The World Next Door: South Asian American Literature and the Idea of America'. Asian American History and Culture. Philadelphia: Temple UP, 2004.
19. Mahapatra, Jayanta & Sharma, Yuyutsu (ed.). Ten: The New Indian Poets. New Delhi: Nirala Publications, 1993.
20. Shivdasani, Menka (ed.). Anthology of Contemp. Indian Poetry : USA, BigBridge.Org, Michael Rothenberg, 2004.
21. Souza, Eunice de. "Nine Indian Women Poets", Delhi, Oxford University Press, 1997.
22. Souza, Eunice de. Talking Poems: Conversations With Poets. New Delhi: Oxford Univ. Press, 1999.
23. Souza, Eunice de. Early Indian Poetry in English: An Anthology: 1829-1947. New Delhi: Oxford Univ. Press, 2005.
24. Meena G.. Khorana; Greenwood (January 2009). The Life and Works of Ruskin Bond. IAP. p. 1–2. ISBN 978-1-60752-075-7.
25. Kumar, Jai (2004-06-24). "Kamala Markandaya". The Guardian. ISSN 0261-3077. Retrieved 2017-03-31.
26. Steve Leblanc Songs of Kobisena 90, PMS Cafe Press, Alston, MS, USA.
27. Jha, Vivekananad. (ed) The Dance of the Peacock. Canada: Hidden Brook Press, 2014.

North-East India and the World : Mahabharata to the advent of Ahoms

Narayan Singh Rao[5]

The Mahabharata war at Kurukshetra was a turning point in the history of Arunachal Pradesh as well as northeast India and the south-east Asia. King Bhagdatta led an army of one *akshauni* which included 109, 350 foot soldiers, 65, 6110 horses, 21,870 charriots, and 21,870 elephants[1]. Most of the soldiers in this army were probably from Arunachal Pradesh as per the description regarding their colour, dress and costumes, style of fighting, etc. given in the Mahabharata. Besides, Bhagdatta and his son Pushpadatta, Rakshasharaj Alambush, Alayuddha, Chitrasena, Dhristketu the king of Chedi (Tezu district of Arunachal Pradesh) alongwith his brother Suketu, Ghatotkacha the king of the area consisting of the parts of upper Assam, Arunachal Pradesh (east) and Nagaland participated in this Great War and made supreme sacrifice in the battle-field to protect their politico-strategic interests[2].

With these great warriors of the time the Adis, the Nishis, the Akas, the Monpas, the Sherdukpons, the Apatanis, the Mishmis living in the princely states of Arunachal Pradesh such as Prabhu Pahar (Subhansiri) Prabhu Kuthar, Vidarbha, Chedi (both located in the Lohit region) Shonitpur (the area earlier dominated by the Akas, the Nishis, the Adis and other kirata tribes of present Arunachal Pradesh) also participated on the either side in the great war at Kurukshetra as they are widely referred as *kiratas*, *mallechas*, etc. who earned reputation for their military prowess, gallantry and the command over sky warfare, war by illusory tactics, magical formulas, space warfare and the use of

---

[5] Professor, Dept. of History, MGSU, Bikane

supernatural powers, etc[3]. When the Kauravas were finally defeated and killed in the battle field of Kurukshetra, the combatants and non-combatants who participated in this war returned back to northeast India and reached to their respective place. Once again, Arjuna followed the horse consecrated for the purpose of *ashwamedha* sacrifice. The King of Pragjyotishpur called Vajradatta the son of Bhagadatta was defeated by Arjuna but he was allowed to retain his Kingdom when he agreed to attend the *Ashwamedha yajna* to be conducted by *Dharmaraja* Yudhisthir at Hastinapur. The king of Manipur, named Babhruvahana, the son of Arjuna accompanied by his mothers Chitrangda and Ulupi were also invited by Arjuna during his visit to Manipur for participation in the *ashwamedha yajna* at Hastinapur[4].

After the death of Ghatotkacha, his son Meghabal Narayan became the new King[5]. Though his name does not figure in the Mahabharata but the sources confirm the fact that he also moved to Hastinapur to attend the biggest ever conclave of the Bhupalas ('Kings') of the entire Indian subcontinent held under the aegis of *Dharmaraja* Yuddhisthir on the occasion of Ashwamedha sacrifice[6]. The kings of northeast India were offered gifts and valuable items by the Pandava brothers at a sending-off ceremony on the eastern gate of Hastinapur[7]. All these events shows that the age of Mahabharata brought all the heroes, great warriors and the kings of northeastern India into the limelight and their contributions in the Mahabharata war will always be remembered by the future generations of our country[8]. Due to geo-strategic location and the presence of major trading and strategic routes the present states of Arunachal Pradesh, Assam, and Manipur continued to enjoy the position of prominence in the history of India.

MIGRATION OF INDIANS AND SPREAD OF HINDU-BUDDHIST CULTURE IN ASIA AND AMERICA

The migration of Indian kshatriyas from the mountainous tract of the northeast India, Myanmar, Southeast Asian region, Far East, China, Russia and America started in the pre-Ramayan and Mahabharata age when Maharishi Parashurama the wielder of exe started the destruction of kshatriyas in order to take revenge for the destruction of his father's asharama by a kshatriya ruler belonging Haihaya clan called Arjuna, the son of Kartvirya. Parshurama killed Arjuna to punish him. However, the sons of Arjuna went to the *ashrama* of Maharishi Jamdagni and killed him by lance and burnt down the *ashrama* when Parashurama was away from the *ashrama*. When Parashurama found his father dead with his head severed brutally by the sons of Arjuna, he vowed to exterminate all kshatriyas and render the entire mother Earth Kshatriya-less. He attacked kshatriyas for repeatedly 21 times and eliminated them completely. At this time, several kshatriyas disguised as women, traders, *shudras* goldsmiths, cow boys, ironsmith, and carpenter etc. to escape from the wrath of Parshurama. Several hordes of kshatriyas of Lunar and Solar race moved to eastern Himalayas i.e. Assam, Manipur, Mizoram, Arunachal Pradesh, Meghalaya, etc. Many of them crossed over the Himalayan Mountain, the Patkai ranges and went to Myanmar, China, Thailand, Cambodia Mongolia, Russia and America to save their life. Several others went into hiding in the jungles of present day Chattisgarh, Jharkhand, Madhaya Pradesh, Aravali hills of Rajasthan, and other parts of the Indian sub-continent. Thus most of the tribes of Arunachal Pradesh probably belong to the solar race of kshatriyas who left the central India to escape from Parshurama. The Adis, the Nishis, the Apatanis, the Monpas, the Sherdukpens, the Akas, the Mishmis etc. come under the category of kshatriyas who moved to Indo-China border and settled there in the present Arunachal Pradesh. The Tutsas, the Tangsas, the Noctes, the Wanchos, the khamtis, the singphos, the Lisus, the Taishans, etc. were probably those kshatriyas who left India in the period between the Parashurama's to the Mahabharata's and settled in China, Mongolia, Southeast Asian region. They moved towards India again when they found that the safety security and means of livelihood are better in their ancestral home. Thus in the early medieval period the trend of migration got reversed. Similarly, the Kols, the Bhils, the Mundas, the Nishadas, the Meenas, and various tribal clans dwelling in the forest were also kshatriyas who went there to hide in jungle to escape from the rishi. The Kshatriya clans also moved towards Russia and landed in America by crossing the Baring strait and got distributed in south and north America. Thus the Hindu civilization, culture and tradition got firmly rooted in the countries located across the globe.

North-East India witnessed the migration of several hordes of kshatriyas, towards Southeast Asia, China, Far East and even beyond[9]. Large number of defeated kings, soldiers, chieftains of the Kshatriya princely states, brahmins, sadhus, and degraded kshatriyas from the Indian mainland crossed the Patkai hills, Myanmar, South China and Southeast Asian region and got settled in almost all the countries across the globe. These people also crossed Barring Strait and reached to America in different batches. It is said that Shukdeo Muni and Maharishi Veda Vyasa visited America by crossing Patkai hills. The probable route followed by them must have passed through Gangadvar, Assam, Pangsao Pass, Arunachal Pradesh, Myanmar (Bhamo), Yunnan (South China) Mongolia, Siberia, Bering strait, Alasca and North and South America[10]. The Hindu civilization got firmly rooted in Siberia (Russia) in pre-Ramayana age as several hordes of the Hindu migrants settled there and assimilated with the locals. It is testified by the fact that Indra (rain god) and Agni (fire god) are worshiped there since several years. There is a practice of sanctifying waters of the local Rivers by chanting holy hymns (*mantras*) and implanting of the Ganga in the same for use in ablutions[11]. The recently discovered idols of Hindu gods and goddesses in Russia pertaining to B.C./A.D. shows that Russian were Hindus since the ancient age[12]. Besides Hinduism, Buddhism also reached to Siberia. Near Baikal Lake (north of Mangolia there are thirty three Buddhist viharas (monasteries) giving training in the Buddhist religion. Mahakal is the deity of Chongal monastery. There is a magnificent idol of Maitreya in Selenga Monastery. Replicas of goddess Saraswati are found in Aginaki monastery. There were Hindu and Buddhist universities like Nalanda of India. The people used to study Vedas, Ashtadhyaya of Panini, Meghadoot of Kalidasa, Ramayana and Mahabharata. Thus, Hindusim reached to Russia via Pangsao pass and the other land routes passing from Arunachal Pradesh Pass[13]. Similarly, the Hindus reached to America[14] by using the International highway passing from the Gangetic plains, east Arunachal Pradesh, Myanmar, China, Mongolia, Siberia, and Bering Strait and the north and south America[15]. The Buddhists later on followed the same route and reached to the American continents[16]. Thus the *Kirata* Kshatriya tribal chieftains of Arunachal Pradesh also played the role of hosts to the Hindus migrating towards the eastern world. The trend of such a migration from India on large scale continued up to 600 CE. However, in the subsequent period i.e. 700 CE onwards several kshatriya clans of Southeast Asia, China and Mongolia started moving back towards India because of the Socio-cultural, economic and political reasons[17].

MIGRATION OF HINDUS VIA PATKAI PASS TO THE SOUTHEAST ASIA

As discussed earlier, Bhagadatta, the hero of northeast India and stalwart military commander of the Kaurava army died like a true Kshatriya alongwith his son Pushpadatta at the hands of Arjuna and thus, the glory and prestige of the empire of Pragjyotishpur was on the path of decay. After this Great War at Kurukshetra, the political climate of the entire Indian sub-continent got deeply influenced by the outcome. A large number of defeated Kshatriya princes, camp followers, attendants, and soldiers migrated to Arunachal Pradesh and finally went to countries of Southeast Asia, China, Mongolia, Russia and America. The Tirap valley also witnessed the large scale migration of the Hindus from south India towards east in the post-Mahabharata period as a section of Andhras, Kalingas, and the Tamils preferred land routes[18]. After the *Mahabharata* war at Kurukshetra, a large number of royal princes, generals, accompanied by their camp followers, retainers, attendants and troops moved to the Southeast Asian region. Thus, the areas located in east and north of Changlang-Tirap and Lauhitya district was completely hinduised. The Lauhitya Pradesh and the Patkai region acted as a kind of bridge between India and Southeast Asia. According to the Burmese chronicles, Kripacharya and *Kula guru* of the Pandavas and the Kauravas fought against Pandavas in Kurukshetra war. Though Kauravas were defeated and got killed in the war, Kripacharya succeeded in assassination of the 5 sons of the Pandavas. He apprehended retaliatory action from the Pandavas and escaped towards Myanmar, got settle down in north-west of the country i.e. Arracan hills by disguising himself as a sanyasi. He became ruler of that area in Arracan hills.

In 800 B.C.E. kshatriyas of Kapilvastu, belonging to Shakya clan, got defeated by royalists, and fled towards *brahmadesha* via Patkai hills as Nepal was connected to Myanmar by an inland trade route. By tracking through the Patkai passes, they descended into upper Myanmar. They founded a Hindu kingdom and ruled there for thirty one generations. Their kingdom was in close proximity of present day Changlang-Tirap and Lohit districts of Arunachal Pradesh. Later on, this Shakya kingdom was destroyed by the Hindu migrants who were ruling over Gandhara rastra, which is also referred as Yun-nan province of China. Shan chronicles refer this area as Nanchao. When the Chinese ruler once again asserted his authority over Nanchao, the Hindus evacuated Gandhara and moved to upper-Myanmar. They attacked the Shakyas and destroyed their kingdom. The Hindus went to Yun-nan province of China and laid foundation of a Hindu kingdom there. This group of people also moved to east from Patkai passes located in east Arunachal Pradesh. There is another tradition which suggests that Shakya kingdom of Myanmar was destroyed by the kshatriyas of Ganga valley. Under the leadership of the son of a Raja of Kashi (Varanasi) the kshatriyas moved to Myanmar via Brahmaputra valley, and sub-Himalayan ranges (possibly Lauhitya or Patkai region) and destroyed the power of Shakyas. Similarly, Hindu kingdoms came into existence in Cambodia. It is mentioned that Adityavamsha king of Hastinapur and his queen Cnandradevi got displeased with their son *rajkumara* Pradyumana and expelled him. The prince nicknamed as Sundara Kumara Pradyumana proceeded towards east by crossing mountains, River valleys and reached Kokathaloka. This country was ruled by a tribal ruler, Naga king who had beautiful daughter. Pradyumana fell in love with the princess and they were allowed to marry. Pradyumana and his descendents played a crucial role in establishing Hindu rule over Cambodia. During this period, the whole of Myanmar, Java, Sumatra, Cambodia, and Vietnam came under the influence of Hindu civilisation and culture. Hindu kingdoms were raised in these countries. Thus, the numerous passes and the *duars* located in Patkai hills, Mishmi hills and the Bhotiya hills of Arunachal Pradesh facilitated the migration of Hindus in the south-east Asian region and even beyond[19].

The Pangsao pass located in Changlang district referred as Khyber pass of the east[20] was one of the most convenient passes through which one can straight way reach the Hwkong valley and move towards Yunan, Mongolia, Thailand.[21] China Russia and America[22]. The Patkai pass (Pangsau pass) linked to Europe, India, Southeast Asia and China. Kajangla (Rajmahal), Pundravardhan (North Bengal) Kamarupa (Gauhati), Upper Assam (Patkai hills) and Bhamo (in Myanmar). From here one could move towards Yun-nan i.e. Kunming which was the chief city of the southern province of China. I-Tsing and Hiuen-Tsang the two Chinese travellers who came to India in the seventh century C.E. mention that twenty Chinese monks had come to India in the middle of third century C.E. via Yun-nan-Myanmar-Assam route. Bamboo sticks, silk and clothes were exported from China to Europe through India. Similarly, a variety of items were brought to China from Bactria via Gangetic plains, Assam, Patkai hills and Myanmar. The Patkai route which leads us to Bhamo and subsequently to China or other south-east Asian countries has been considered as most practical line of communication from Assam to China by the British. As mentioned earlier, strategic highways in Patkai ranges of east Arunachal Pradesh linked the whole of Southeast Asia,[23] China, Russia and America with India[24].

MIGRATION OF THE HINDUS AND THE BUDDHISTS OF SOUTH-EAST ASIA TOWARDS INDIA

The rise Nalanda and Vikramshila universities and the emergence of the several other centres of learning in ancient India attracted lakhs of students, scholars and Buddhist monks who undertook journey towards India from China, Japan, Thailand Myanmar, Vietnam, Russia, Malaya, Indonesia and almost all countries of the eastern world. The intake of teachers and the students in these universities substantially went up when Buddhism reached Southeast Asia and the Far East. Generally, the students and the teachers from Southeast Asia reached India via Tirap valley and the Patkai hills. The land route from Yunnan province of China moved along the northern Myanmar and this route took the *bhikshus* and the students to Nalanda University via Arunachal Pradesh and Assam. This was the shortest route in term if the volume of time taken and the logistics required for taking the journey via sea route. The migration from the Southeast Asia and Far East to India, for the purpose of study of Hindu religion, philosophy, astronomy Buddhism, Jainism, Sanskrit, Pali, Prakrit, etc. continued up to the Sultanate period when these world renowned universities were destroyed and burnt down by Muhammed Bakhtiyar Khalji the commander of the Sultan Muizzuddin Muhammed of Ghauri in 1202-3[25]. The Muslim invader ordered wholesale murder of the Buddhist monks, Brahmins, the students and the teachers. Millions of valuable books, manuscripts, *shastras*, etc. were burnt down[26]. This destruction and armed attack on the universities compelled lakhs of students studying there to once again rush back to Southeast Asia. The Brahmins, the Buddhist bhikshus, scholars, teachers, etc. moved towards Assam and by taking the route of Pangsao Pass in Patkai hills. They descended in the northern Myanmar at Bhamo and subsequently reached to Yunan. From here they got distributed in different countries of the Southeast Asia Far East, China and Russia[27]. Thus the migration from India to the countries of the eastern world is a process which started in the *prehistoric* period[28]. The Arunachal Pradesh which served as gateway to the eastern world played a crucial role in the dissemination of Indian culture and civilization across the globe[29].

NORTH EAST INDIA DURING THE AGE OF THE MAURYAS AND THE GUPTAS

It is suggested by the evidences that interaction of Indian communities with the people of Myanmar (across the Patkai hills) became stronger and meaningful between 1000-600 BCE[30]. During the period of Maurya's a large number of defeated princes migrated to Myanmar[31]. Buddhist monks and Brahmins also moved to Southeast Asia and propagated Buddhism and Hinduism[32]. Lust of gold, precious stones, and wealth attracted adventurers, merchants and traders towards the east[33]. The 300 C.E. witnessed the advent of Gupta dynasty on the political map of northern India. Chandragupta and Samudragupta organized military expeditions and incorporated the whole of eastern India into their empire. According to *Raghuvamsham* of Kalidas, the ruler of Pragjyotishpur submitted before Gupta emperor and accepted them as their overlord by paying tribute.

The rule of Naraka dynasty came to an end in 4th century C.E. A prince, who traced his descent from Naraka Bhagdatta line, known as Pushyavarman became founder of Varman dynasty. He was contemporary of Chandragupta and Samudragupta. Pushyavarman was succeeded by his son Samudravarman. At this time Samudragupta adopted a policy of aggressive warfare and military conquest. He imposed subsidiary alliance upon the rulers of *pratyanta* ('frontier') states. According to Allahabad pillar inscription, entering into such alliances required the lesser chiefs to pay annual tribute and express obedience to the commands and pay homage to paramount ruler by personally attending the court of Guptas. The ruler of Pragjyotishpur might have initially resisted such a move of the Gupta emperor, but the mighty Guptas too were determined to establish their hold over north-eastern part of India. Kalidas, in *Raghuvamsham*, mentions that when Lord Raghu crossed the Lauhitya River (Brahamaputra), the Lord of Pragiyotish began to tremble in fear, but he later pleased the advancing conqueror by paying him homage and presenting excellent war elephants. Thus, Samudragupta organized a successful military expedition and pushed boundaries of his kingdom up to Lauhitya and Patkai regions. The submission of Samudravarman before the Gupta king is confirmed by Nidhanpur plates which state that Kamrupa king was rich enough to gratify the Gupta overlord with precious articles of gift and tribute and saved his kingdom from being annexed to Gupta empire[34]. However, the acceptance of the Gupta over-lordship by Kamrupa king indirectly brought the entire territory from Kartoya to Lauhitya and Patkai (east Arunachal Pradesh and northern Myanmar) ranges within the boundaries of Gupta empire. The evidences contained in Burmese chronicles, supported by archeological evidences, inform us that Samvat and Gupta calendars were in use in the kingdom of

Bhukama (which later on became Pagan). The discovery of a stone slab bearing Gupta era dates, in the kingdom of Pagan, shows that Burmese rulers accepted over-lordship of Samudragupta[35]. Hindu influence was also strongly evident in Gandhara rashtra (south China) where kshatriyas were ruling since first century BCE. All these suggest that boundaries of the Gupta Empire extended up to Myanmar and borders of China[36]. Naturally the whole of east Arunachal Pradesh became part and parcel of the same. The Patkai ranges served as a linkage between India and Myanmar.

NORTH EAST INDIA IN THE AGE OF YASHOVERMAN AND HARSHA

The Gupta dynasty came to an end in 510 CE as the last Gupta ruler Bhanugupta was defeated by the Hunas who attacked north-western frontier under the leadership of Mihirkula who ruled over north-west India from 525-530 CE. The Hunas were challenged by Yashodharman of Malwa. He defeated the Hunas and took over the control of territory held by Gupta rulers. According to Mandsor inscriptions C.I.I. No. 533-34, the armies of Yashodharman marched towards east and west, compelled *samantas* ('feudal lords') of different parts of India from Lauhitya (Brahamaputra) in the east to western ocean and from the Himalayas in north to the Mahendra mountain in the south, to accept him as their overlord. The extent of Yashodharman's empire up to *Lauhitya Sagara* proves that he exercised authority over Kamrupa, upper Assam, and east Arunachal Pradesh. Kamrupa's king Bhutivarman accepted Yashodharman as his overlord[37].

The prominent successors of Bhutivarman were Chandramukhvarman (555-565 C.E.), Sthitavarman (565-585 C.E.) and Bhaskarvarman (c. 594-650 C.E.). The last one is considered as remarkable and brilliant king of Kamrupa. He was contemporary of Harsha and possessed various qualities of head and heart. He forged a military alliance with

Harshvardhan and defeated Raja Sasanka of Gauda (Bengal). Bhaskarvarman, the king of Pragjyotisha, was given high degree of respect and was treated equal in status by Harsha. A remarkable event of that time was the visit of Chinese traveler Yunan Chwang to the north-east India. Later on, Bhaskarvarman accompanied Yuan Chwang to the court of Harsha in Kannauja. Both attended Buddhist council convened by Harsha at Prayag. After the conclusion of Buddhist council Yuan Chwang came to Pragjyotishpur and wrote widely on the northeast India[38] while giving an account of geography and socio-cultural life of this region he states, "On the east, Kamrupa is bounded by a line of hills so there is no great city in the kingdom. The frontiers are contiguous to the barbarians of south-west China. These tribes are in fact akin to those of the Man people (i.e. the south-west barbarians) in their customs".

These remarks of the Chinese traveler are of far reaching significance for the purpose of the reconstruction of the history of Arunachal Pradesh. Firstly, the kingdom of Pragjyotishpur extended up to south-west China and there was no independent state between Kartoya in the west to China borders in the east. It is also proved that present Arunachal Pradesh was part of the kingdom of Pragjyotishpur. The Chinese chronicles have also stated that Bhaskarvarman, a contemporary of Harsha, is referred as king of eastern India. *Yogini Tantra* further strengthens the point that king Bhaskara's kingdom extended from Kartoya in the west to Dikkarvasini in the east[39]. King Bhaskara maintained cordial relationship with Chinese rulers. The account of Tang dynasty of China proves that Chinese rulers exchanged diplomatic missions with Harsha, a friend and contemporary of Bhaskarvarman. The third Chinese mission headed by Wang-Hiuen-Tse reached Kannauja in 647-48 CE when Harsha had already died. The Chinese diplomat was ill-treated by Arjuna who had usurped the throne of Harsha's kingdom. In order to teach a lesson to Arjuna, Wang-Hiuen-Tse sought armed assistance of

Bhaskarvarman. He collected 1000 Tibetan and 7000 Nepalese troops, and 30,000 elephants and horses of Bhaskara. He attacked and defeated the usurper and imprisoned him. Thus, Bhaskarvarman was one of the most illustrious rulers of India[40].

With the decline of the Varman dynasty, another group of Kiratas took over the control of Brahmaputra valley and territories of Kamrupa. Their leader was called Salastambha, who traced his descent from Bhagadatta. By taking advantage of the declining power of Varman dynasty, and prevailing lawlessness, he captured the throne in 655 C.E. People, who resisted the growing influence of Buddhism, supported Salastambha to organise rebellion to protect indigenous culture and tradition. Salastambha died in 675 C.E. and he was succeeded by a line of twenty kings, the last one among them was Tyag Singha. Prominent ruler of this dynasty was Harshadeva who occupied Bengal, Bihar, Orissa, Andhra, Northern Tamil Nadu and Kosala. His kingdom extended from Ayodhya in west to China border in the east. Uttarkol, Dakhinkol, Lauhitya and Patkai region were part of his kingdom. Next rulers were Salamba (Pralamba) and Harrajvarman. Later adopted high sounding titles such as Maharajadhiraja, Parmeshwara; Parambhattaraka; etc. and promoted Vedic culture. He also shifted capital to Tejpur. Next important rulers were Vanmala, Varmandeva, Balavarman III and Tyag. Singha[41]. Salastambas were worshipper of *Hetukasulin* (Shiva). Great Vedantist reformers and Hindu philosophers visited Kamrupa, and entered into debate with Abhinav Gupta.

Trade and commerce also flourished during this period. In the 10th century C.E. the Salastamba dynasty came to an end. A prince of Narkasur line, called Brahamapala, founded Pala dynasty. Ratanapala was prominent ruler of this line of kings. Palas ruled for about 200 years and in 13th century the kingdom of Kamrupa started disintegrating.

Petty states assumed independence. Successive Muslim invasions speeded up this decaying of the kingdom of Kamrupa[42]. A branch of Kirata (Chautiya) kshtriyas headed by Satyanarayan and Laxminarayan took over the control of area between Sisi in the west to Brahmakunda in the east, on the north by hills and in the south by Buri Dihing. The Kirata Kshatriya clans who lived and dominated the politics of Assam and Arunachal Pradesh were the Bodos, the Kacharis, and the Chutiyas. In the ancient period, the Kirata chiefs of Shonitpur, Hidimbapur, Dimapur, Chedi, Vidarbha Prabhu, Kuthar, Lohitya region, Prabhu Pahar (once ruled by Hiranyakashyap and Prahlada) located in Subaansiri River valley etc. were independent kingdoms in the ancient times[43]. Later on, occasionally they might have accepted the over-lordship of the king of Pragjyotishpur. Most of the Kings of northeast India demonstrated respect towards the king of Pragjyotisha/Kamarupa because of its historical significance, strategic location and military strength.

Raja Bhagdatta of Pragjyotishpur and his predecessor Narakasur emerged as the legendry figures and they played significant role in the age of Mahabharata and Ramayana. In the Mahabharata and *Puranas*, Bhagdatta is considered as leader of the coalition of the kings of entire eastern India who challenged Krishna through Shishupala and Jarasandh. Rukma, the brother of Rukmani. Later on Bhagdatta joined the Kauravas alongwith *Kirata* and the Chin soldiers. Thus, due to power, prestige and the glory of the kingdom of Pragjyotisha/Kamarupa, all the chief of northeastern India accepted nominal command of the king of Kamarupa[44]. Of course, whenever the power and prestige of the king of Pragjyotishpur was on decline, the local Kirata chiefs of Assam and Arunachal Pradesh might have became autonomous[45]. The Tutsa, the Tangsa, and the Nocte oral literature refers the terms *Fisa, Bodo, Hellons*, etc. confirming the presence of some kirata people in the Tirap valley when the Tangsas and the Nocte, the Tutsas etc. started pouring in to the area in 12th century. There were also occasions when the Tangsas, the Tutsas, and others had to face armed attack of Kirata tribes[46]. The kirata, the Cinas and the Mahacinas controlled a vast tract extending from south-west of China to Kartoya in the west, Tibet in the north and sea coast (Bay of Bengal) in the south. Pragjyotishpur was ruled over by the Kirata chiefs. With the decline of Harsha's empire and subsequent decay of the authority of Pragjyotishpur in the 10th century C.E.[47], the Kirata clans started migrating westward. Many Kirata chieftains carved out independent states in upper Assam. The Chutiyas and the Kacharis concentrated themselves in Brahmaputra valley. Swaadhyayapuri (Sadiya)[48] and Dimapur (Heidamkapur) emerged as alternative centres of power. Dimasa Bodos are the descendent of Bhimsen Pandava who got married to Hedimba the daughter of chief of the republic of Hairambajanad. Bhima's son through Heidamba called Ghatotkacha is considered as the great ancestor of the Bodos.

There were about 182 rulers in this dynasty. The last one was Raja Govind Chandra Narayan whose kingdom was annexed by the British government in the first part of nineteenth century[49]. The Bhuiyans also emerged as powerful ruling class on the northern bank of Brahmaputra, and subsequently the Koches (another Kirata Kshatriya clan) also appeared on the political map of eastern India, and in 1515 C.E. an independent Koch kingdom was established. The migration of the Kiratas from parts of Arunachal Pradesh gained momentum when the Taishans and several Tangsa clans were knocking at the gate of our eastern frontier. When Shan Prince Hsoka-Hpa (Sukapha) crossed the Patkai hills and entered in present Changlang district, he encountered a great number of Kacharis (Bodos). From them he came to know that Kachari Raja was defeated by tribes of the area so he had to surrender Mohong to the latter and retreat to the side of Dikhow River. The Ahom *Buranjis* confirm this fact that Bodo/Kachari kingdom was extended up to the Patkai hills. The Bodo Kacharis were so powerful at that time that even Sukapha hesitated in attacking them. He preferred to not antagonise the Kacharis. He first subjugated Moran Borahies and did not confront the Kacharis at all during his life time.

In 1215 C.E. onwards, the Ahoms and the Tangsas, the Noctes, and the Tutsas succeeded in establishing their hegemony over Patkai hills, the plains of Nao Dihing, Buri Dihing and Tirap valley. The Bodos, the Kacharis and other Kirata clans were pressurised to evacuate these areas and move towards the plains of Brahmaputra. The Kiratas raised powerful kingdoms there[50], and also continued their migration towards north-western and central India, and played crucial role in the formation of Rajput states in Madhya Pradesh, Rajasthan and other provinces of northern India[51].

MIGRATION OF INDIANS AND FOUNDATION OF HINDU KINGDOMS IN SOUTH-EAST ASIA AND CHINA :

The first wave of migration of the kshatriyas towards northeast India and Southeast Asia was started in pre-Ramayana age. Maharishi Parshurama, the wielder of axe, undertook a vow to eliminate kshatriyas as they had allegedly deviated from the path of truth, righteousness and failed in upholding dharma. When Parshurama's axe caused death and destruction everywhere, many kshatriyas disguised as Brahmins, *sanyasis*, bards, and even women[52] retried into the thickly forested areas of north-east India to escape from the wrath of the angry sage[53]. Possibly, a large number of such kshatriyas even crossed mountain ranges and reached up to Myanmar, China, Thailand, Cambodia and several other parts of the world.

The evidences suggest that Hindu civilisation and culture flourished in countries of Southeast Asia during the epic age. The Kiratas, the Cinas, the Mahacinas, the Mlechhas, the Yavanas the Adis, the Akas, the Mishmis, the Monpas the Sherdukpens, the Nishis, and the Mishings participated in Mahabharata war at Kurukshetra. Puranas, Vedas and other categories of ancient literature contained names, location and other details about countries of Southeast Asia and northeast India. The process of migration of the Hindus via east Arunachal Pradesh (Patkai hills) towards Southeast Asia got accelerated in post-Mahabharata period. Large number of Hindu princes accompanied by armed retainers, traders, Brahmins, etc. moved to the east. The Chinese chronicles suggest that India was effectively linked to China through an overland route. The Chinese travelers used to visit India via Patkai hills and Lohit region without any fear of the Kiratas and other communities. The Hindu migrants who reached Southeast Asia and China founded Hindu kingdoms and played a crucial role in firmly planting the flag of Indian civilization on the Patkai-Myanmar-Nan-Chao route. Once the route was cleared, the merchants, traders and religious scholars also took it to go to the east. These migrants acted as torch-bearers of Indian civilization in the eastern world. With missionary zeal Indians crossed difficult mountains, Rivers, thick forests infested with wild poisonous animals and stepped into the valleys of Irrawaddy, Mekong and Yang-tse-Kiang. Hindu colonies sprang up in Myanmar, Nan-Chao (Gandhara), Vietnam, Siam, Laos and Cambodia.

The descriptions about the difficult geographical conditions faced by migrants are identical to the geography and climate of east Arunachal Pradesh. It is mentioned that the migrants had to climb up and down, and jump like frog[54], and keep stick in hands to cross steep slopes. Such routes are mentioned as *vetrapatha*. The travelers had to cross mighty Rivers. With the help of bamboo made rafts and bridges constructed to cross Rivers. Such portions of the route were called as *vamshapatha*. People used to cook food on their way, using wet wood and bamboo which used to cause huge cloud like smoke. This attracted the attention of the Kiratas who used to attack unaware wayfarers, kill them and enjoy their flesh. Sometimes bloody conflicts also used to take place between the Kiratas and the migrants. The people on migration had to pass through jungle thickets without any track and sleep on rocks where no human being had put his foot before. The route heading towards east was infested by poisonous snakes, scorpions, leeches, etc. creeping on the ground and falling like rain drops from tall trees and sucking human blood. Such portions of the route are referred as *vishapath* ('poisonous track') and *raktapatha* ('the bloody path'). Such tracks were generally very narrow enabling only one person to pass at a time and a group had to move in a single file. On the way, temporary huts of bamboo were raised. The migrants were required to quickly leave such stations to escape from attacks of the Kiratas.

A perennial stream of human migration from India, through Patkai Lohit and Mishmi hills flowed into the valleys of Irrawaddy, Mekong, and Yang-Tse-Kiang, since pre-Ramayana period to 10th century C.E.[55]. The hordes of migrants from northwestern India, central India and the Gangetic plains first moved to Assam plains, crossed hills of Arunachal Pradesh or Manipur, and en-route they recruited men from Kirata clans as soldiers, attendants etc. On their arrival they raised settlements in the country of their destination. There is strong probability that the migrants after crossing the Patkai hills, landed at Bhamo in Myanmar. From here one route led towards Nan-Chao (Gandhara), China proper and Vietnam, Cambodia and Hindu kingdom of Indrapura was established[56].

In Myanmar (south of Changlang) a prince of Hastinapur founded a Hindu kingdom called Srikshetra. Its capital was also called Hastinapur which was subsequently shifted to Bhumawati, also known as Bhukama. This dynasty ruled up to 483 B.C.E. and another prince of Hastinapur, Dasharath, came to Myanmar. He attacked Bhumawati and captured the throne. His descendents ruled over Bhumawati up to 108 B.C.E. This ruling family too was eliminated by the Hindus who retreated from Gandhara (Nan-Chao) because of pressure mounted against them by the Chinese authorities. The Gandhara Rathas captured Bhumawati, shifted capital to Bhukama, and finally it became Pagan[57]. A stone slab discovered by Fuhrar proves that Gupta samwat (era) was used by Myanmarese rulers for official purposes. It also suggests that Gupta rulers were accepted as paramount chief by rulers of Myanmar. Hindus had developed strong politico-cultural and commercial contacts with the people of China and Southeast Asia in the early period of our history[58].

The Hindus and the Buddhists settled in northern Myanmar were so endeared to the local people that they used the term *Priya* ('dear') while referring them. The Burmese chronicles use the term *Brahamadesha* for northern Myanmar. The Pyus or Priyas were those who were born of Indian father and Burmese mother. The Pyu inscriptions are written in Kadamba script of Konkan coast and Goa. It shows that Pyus reached Myanmar overland route through Patkai hills. The Chinese chronicles state that in Hamwaza capital of Pyu kingdom, Hinduism and Buddhism co-existed and flourished. The Shakyas under the leadership of Abhiraja of Kapilvastu migrated to Myanmar and founded a Hindu kingdom which survived for thirty one generations. This kingdom was destroyed by the kshatriyas of Ganga valley. In 146 C.E. Chandra Surya, a prince of Varanasi, took over the control of Arakan hills, and made Dharmawati the capital. His dynasty ruled up to 780 C.E. Similarly, the Kaliga's founded kingdom of Kulashthana and the Mauryas of Patliputra settled between Bhamo and Tagung. The Telgus, also referred as Talings or Ramannadesha, settled at the mouth of Salwin and coast of Martban and founded Hindu kingdom there. In the same manner, kingdoms of Champapura, Sanvi, Utkalpa and Santabhya were established by the people who migrated to Myanmar from different parts of India[59]. This trend of human migration towards east from India continued up to 12th century wherein east Arunachal Pradesh played important role. The area of present Changlang district, once upon a time, remained part of the empire of Pandavas, the Guptas and the Yashodharman and acted as India's gateway to Southeast Asia. Thus, in view of these evidences we can safely conclude that the present Changlang and Tirap districts of Arunachal Pradesh have played noteworthy role in the history of India.

We have discussed the migration of Indians towards Southeast Asia, China, and the Far East, a phase that started in pre-Ramayana age and continued up to 12th century C.E. This phase came to an end due to several factors. Firstly, the northwestern India was attacked by the Muslims; several Rajput kingdoms were destroyed; towns and cities were ruined; and educational institutions were burnt down. People lost courage and strength to venture out. Secondly, the politics in Southeast Asia also got seriously affected by the movement of the Taishans from Mongolia. They moved to south China, occupied major parts of Myanmar and finally targeted Brahmaputra valley. Thus, an important overland route connecting India and Southeast Asia came under the control of the Taishans. The Shan rulers were adventurous and possessed superior military technology and weaponry. There was no strong political power in the northeast India, like Bhagdatta's, to check the onward march of the Taishan leader Sukapha (Hso-Ka-Hpa). Thirdly, the migration of the Taishans, and the conflict between various states on the one hand and the Shan rulers on the other created the problem of lawlessness. The wealth of the region got exhausted and it could no longer attract people to migrate towards east. Political crises in Southeast Asian countries reached a stage where everyone looked towards to India as fertile ground for fulfilling their political ambitions. Consequently, a trend reversal in migration began in 1200 C.E. and now people from east started moving towards the India. For the

Taishans, the Tangsas, the Noctes, the Tutsas, the Khamtis, and the Singphos, it was like home coming. These communities had considerable amount of Indian (or Hindu) blood in their veins and they brought unique socio-political and cultural institutions to our country and enriched our heritage and national culture. The people of India who migrated in a big way to east got mixed with indigenous communities, established cordial relationship, got married with local girls and completely assimilated with the society there. However the migration of the Taishans, the Tangsas, and the Tutsas in Patkai and Brahmaputra valley is very significant.

References :
1. Vasu N.N. *The Social History of Kamrupa* Vol. I, Delhi, 1990, pp. 120-33.
2. Veda Vyasa, Manamahirishi, *Mahabharata* Vol. III. Geeta Press, Gorakhpur 2060 v.s. pp. 2483-2485, 2952-2960, 2980-3007; Vol. IV Ghatotkacha Vadha Parva 3550-3667.
3. *Ibid.*
4. *Ibid* Volume VI, Ashwameghik Parva pp. 6252-62, 62-64-6276, 6284-6293.
5. Rao, S, Krishna, Mahabharata Kal Se Chale Aa Rahe Uttar Purvanchal Ke Ye Chandra Vanshi Raj Kul Kya Tribal Thai? Dhurt Angrejo Ke Jhuth Ka Bhanda Phodd (in Hindi), *Hindu Chetna*, April 1984, pp. 13-17.
6. *Ibid.* Also see reference 4.
7. Veda Vyasa Manmahirishi *op. cit.*, Vol. VI, pp. 6290 – 6293.
8. *Ibid.* Vol. I, Heidimbha Vadha Parva, pp. 452-467; Arjuna Vanavasa Parva, pp. 613-617; Digvijaya Parva, pp. 741-752; Raj Suya Parva, pp. 766-838; Vol. II, Tirth Yatra, pp. 1345-1353; Vol. III Rathati Rath Sankhyan Parva, pp. 2479-2492, Bhishma Vadhparva, pp. 2900-2905; 2956-2960, 2980-2996; Vol. IV Shansptak Vadha Parva, pp. 3179-3187; Jayadrath Vadhparva, pp. 3384-3387, 3430-3434; Ghatotkacha Vadha Parva, pp. 3550-3663; Karna Vadha Parva, pp. 3763-3769; Strivilap Parva, pp. 4412-4414; Vol. VI, pp. 6252-6303. The role of the great kings, and the warriors from the northeast India, who contributed in the war between the Pandavas and the Kauravas as well as other related events which took place in the age of Mahabharata is widely discussed in most of the chapters of Mahabharata. No other region of India is given importance as much as given to (the heros of) Assam, Arunachal Pradesh, Nagaland and Manipur. Thus northeast India played a crucial role in the politics of Indian subcontinent in the age of Mahabharata.
9. Ved Vyasa, Mahirishi, op. cit. Vol. V, pp. Rajdharma-Anushashan Parva, pp. 4541-4548, Sathe, Sri Ram, *Saga of India's interaction with world*, 1999; *Antiquity and Greatness of Bharath*, Mysore 1997. *World civilizations: Two Views – Two expansions Hyderabad*, 2000, Jain, Krishna Lal, *Hindu Raj in the World*, New Delhi, 1989, pp. 69-133.
10. *Ibid.*
11. Sathe, Sri Ram, *World civilizations: Two views two expansions*, Hyderabad 2000, pp. 25-26.

12. Roos (Russia) Me Bhi Puje Jate They Bhagwan Vishnu, *Navbharat Times* New Delhi January 5, 2007; Roos (Russia) Ke Gaon Me Mili Vishnu Pratima *Dainik Jagran*, New Delhi, January 5, 2007.
13. Sathe Sri Ram, – *The Saga of India's interaction with the world*, Hyderabad 1999, pp. 43-44.
14. Hebalkar, Sharad, *Essays on History of pre-Colombian America*, Ambajogai, 2002.
15. Sathe, Sri Ram *op. cit.*
16. Hebalkar, Sharad, *op. cit.;* pp. 26, 97-98.
17. Rao, Narayana Singh, *Tribal culture, Faith, History and Literature,* New Delhi, 2006, pp. 93-155.
18. The Kalings and the Andhras referred as *Ramannadesha* founded the Hindu kingdom in Burma with capital at Hansavati/Hansadwipa in the Valley of Salwin River. Similarly, the people from Andhra and Kalingadesha of India moved to Thailand via land route and established the kingdom of Alvirastra there with the backing of emperor Samudragupta. Another batch of the Hindus from Southeastern India laid foundation of the kingdom of Dvarawati by moving to Thailand through land route passing from Arunachal Pradesh and Assam.
19. Kanchan, R.K. *op. cit.;* pp. 23-26.
20. Barua, Hem. *The Red River & The Blue Hill*, Guwahati, 1991, p. 2.
21. Lahiri, Nayanjot. *Pre-Ahom Assam*, New Delhi, 1991, pp. 148-167.
22. Sathe, Sriram, *op. cit.;* Also see, Jain Krishna Lal *Hindu Raj in the World*, New Delhi, 1989, pp. 117-132.
23. Cosh, J.M. On the various lines of overland communication between India and China; *Proceedings of the Royal Geographical Society of London*, Vol. p. 49.
24. Jain, Krishna Lal *op. cit.;* pp. 117-132.
25. Sathe, Sriram, *op. cit.;* Jain, Krishna Lal *op. cit.;* Hebalkar, *op. cit.*
26. Majumdar, R.C. *Ancient India* New Delhi, 1987, pp. 476-493.
27. Gogoi, Padmeshwar, *The Tai and the Tai Kingdoms.*
28. Kanchan, R.K. *The Hindu Kingdoms of South East Asia* pp. 102-105.
29. Lahiri, Nayanjot, *op. cit.;* pp. 148-167.
30. Kanchan, R.K. *op. cit.;* 1990, pp.23-26.
31. *Ibid* pp. 48-86.
32. Lahiri, Nayanjot, *op. cit.;* pp. 148-167.
33. Kanchan, R.K. *op. cit.;* pp. 45-70.
34. Basak, R.G. *History of North-Eastern India*, Calcutta, 1965, pp. 182-185.
35. Kanchan, R.K. *op. cit.;* pp. 84-89
36. Majumdar, R.C. *Hindu Colonies in the Far East,* Calcutta, 1991; pp. 256-260.
37. Sircar, D.C. *Studies in the Geography of Ancient and Medieval India*, New Delhi, 1971.
38. Barua S.L. *A Comprehensive History of Assam*, New Delhi, 1985, pp. 98-109.
39. Yogini Tantra (ed. K.M. Bhattacharjya), Bombay 1925.
40. Barua, S.L. *op. cit.*
41. *Ibid*, p. 110-113.
42. *Ibid.* p. 121-128.
43. Osik, N.N. *A Brief History of Arunachal Pradesh*, New Delhi, 1996, pp. 16-31.
44. Veda Vyasa; *Mahabharata*, Vol. I Rajsuarambha Parva, pp. 706-721, Digvijaya Parva, pp. 741-745. *Ibid.* Mahabharat Khil Bhag Hari Vansha, *Shri Hari Vansha Purana*, Gorakhpur 2060 v.s. pp. 550-557. For details see *Vishnu Parv*, pp. 260-915.
45. Momin, M. Urbanisation in Brahamaputra Valley, Circa AD 600-1200, *Archaeology of North Eastern India* (Ed. Singh, Jaiprakash & Sengupta, Gautam) New Delhi, 1991, p. 262-63.

46. Barua, S.N. *Tribes of Indo Myanmar Border*, New Delhi 1991, p. 42.
47. Choudhary, J.N. Pre-Historic and Early Tribal Migrations in North-Eastern India (Ed. Singh Jaiprakash & Sengupta Gautam *op. cit.*) New Delhi, 1991, p. 86.
48. Gait, Edward, *A History of Assam*, Guwahati, 1997, pp. 38-39.
49. Sapre, Krishna Damodar. Bodo Janajati Ki Gauravshali Parampara, *Bappa Raval*, October-November (4) (year not mentioned).
a. Also see, Krishna Rao, S. Mahabharat Kal Se Chale Aaa Rahe Uttar Purvanchal Ke Ye Chandravanshi Rajkul Kya Tribal They? Dhurt Angrejo Ke Jhuth Ka Bhanda Phod, *Hindu Chetna*, New Delhi, April, 1994, pp, 13-18.
50. L Devi, *Ahom Tribal Relations*, Guwahati, 1992, p. 92.
51. Probably the Agnikula kshatriyas were a mixture of the Kiratas, the Taishans and other solar and lunar tribes of northeast India.
52. Tod, James, *Annals and Antiquities of Rajasthan*, Vol. III, Delhi, 1993 p. 1442.
53. Nath, D. *History of the Koch Kingdom, 1515-1615*, Delhi, 1989, pp. 5-6.
54. Majumdar R.C. *Hindu Colonies in the Far East*, Calcutta, 1991, pp. 8-32.
55. *Ibid.*
56. Kanchan R.K. *op. cit.;* pp. 83-110
57. *Ibid.*
58. *Ibid.*
59. *Ibid.*

India's Greatest Pravasi Mahatma
A person who changed the lives of millions for the better.

Rupanuga Das

For many decades, the United States of America has been a magnet for immigrants from all over the world. An overwhelming majority of these people have come for economic reasons (to raise the standard of living for themselves and their children), or for reasons of personal safety. Some have come for higher studies, with their final goal to avail better employment and business opportunities in America and improve their financial status. A significant percentage of these immigrants have settled down nicely in the USA and made significant contributions to the country and the American society in areas such as finance, technology, engineering, medicine, and arts & culture. They have added to the diversity of the country having imported many of their traditions, festivals, and recipes. Some prominent names in this category are Albert Einstein, Audrey Hepburn, Henry Kissinger, Joseph Pulitzer, Christiane Amanpour, Anand Krishna, Sunder Pichai and Satya Nadella.

In 1965, an ascetic from India came to the USA for completely different reasons. His name was A.C. Bhaktivedanta Swami. In 1968, his American disciples convinced him to allow them to use the title of Srila Prabhupada for him, which is a title for a most exalted Guru, or spiritual teacher. Since that time, he has been addressed as His Divine Grace A.C. Bhaktivedanta Swami Srila Prabhupada or Srila Prabhupada in short.

"Srila" is a term used for a person worthy of our utmost respect and reverence and its literal meaning is *"one who is invested with both beauty and the power to understand the līlā (pastimes) of Kṛṣṇa."* Prabhupada means *one who is always found at the Lotus Feet of Krishna (the Supreme Master).*

Arriving in the United States During the Counterculture Movement

Srila Prabhupada did not come to the USA for any personal gain, be that economic or a desire for fame and prestige. He came to execute the instruction of his Guru to share Krishna Consciousness in the west and to fulfill the prophecy of Lord Chaitanya (an incarnation of Lord Krishna, who appeared in India about 530 years ago) that one day in all villages and towns around the world, Krishna's name will be chanted. Once, he was asked in London, England, why he had come there. His response was, "You came to India 250 years ago and looted and pilfered all its valuables. But you missed one extremely valuable thing; that is the knowledge of our scriptures and the holy name of

Lord Krishna. Now I have come here on my own to give you that for free." This was his motivation and mood – simply to give the knowledge of the scriptures and the holy name of Sri Krishna to anyone who was interested. He did not care if the recipients were rebelling against their authority, were high on drugs, ate meat or drank alcohol or enjoyed unrestricted sex. Almost a 100% of his American followers in the beginning were "hippies." He was convinced that the knowledge of scriptures and the chanting of the holy name would deliver all from the miseries of life.

In the mid sixties, around the same time as Srila Prabhupada's arrival, many other swamis and yogis had come to America and had tried to establish themselves as religious leaders. Some preached the practice of yoga and had some degree of success. Others tried to preach concocted philosophies and had less than limited success. Srila Prabhupada, on the other hand, had unparalleled success in accomplishing his mission of spreading Krishna's name. His purity and devotion allowed him to establish Krishna Consciousness as it is, without being watered down. After establishing a number of temples, farm communities and bhakti centres in various cities in America and Canada, he started to travel around the globe and successfully attracted followers in almost every country in the world, including communist countries like the former Soviet Union, Hungary and Ukraine, Muslim countries like UAE, Bahrain, Malaysia and Pakistan, atheistic countries like China, and of course, India. He established more than 100 temples and farm communities and inspired thousands of people in these countries to devote their lives to Krishna Consciousness. He initiated around 10,000 disciples, who vowed to take to Krishna Consciousness seriously, including following the four regulative principles of no meat eating, no intoxication including cigarettes, tea and coffee, no illicit sex, and no gambling. These disciples would wake up around 3:30 AM every day to participate in their daily devotional activities. They gave up their former "hippy" lifestyle completely, and enjoyed the bliss of Krishna Consciousness.

History of Srila Prabhupada

Srila Prabhupada was born in a Vaishnava (devotees of Lord Vishnu) family in Calcutta and was named Abhay Charan Dey. Right from early childhood he preferred to visit a temple rather than play with his friends. He graduated from Scottish Church College in Calcutta in 1920 with majors in English, Philosophy, and Economics. However, he refused to accept his diploma, in protest to the British, and in congruence with the budding Indian independence movement.

In 1922, he first met a prominent scholar of Gaudiya Vaishnava principles and founder of 64 Gaudiya temples, Srila Bhaktisiddhanta Saraswati Goswami. This Swami asked him to preach Vedic knowledge in the English language throughout the western world. Initially, Abhay replied with, "India needs to gain its independence first, and then we can share Indian knowledge around the world." Srila Bhaktisiddhanta told him, "The message of Krishna Consciousness is too urgent to wait." This deeply impressed Abhay. In 1933, he took initiation from Goswami ji and officially became his disciple. In 1944, he started a publication called 'Back to Godhead' from his home in Calcutta, which aimed at spreading Krishna

Consciousness. He was the magazine's sole writer, designer, publisher, editor, copy editor and distributor.

For three years, he toiled to spread knowledge about the grace of Lord Krishna through his magazine and suffered severe physical hardships in his quest to popularize the publication. His efforts were recognized by the Gaudiya Vaishnava Society in 1947 and he was conferred the title 'Bhaktivedanta,' meaning "one who has realised that devotional service to the Supreme Lord *is* the end of all knowledge." From then on he was known as Bhaktivedanta Swami. He retired from married life at the age of 54 in 1950. After four years, he adopted the 'vanaprastha' (retired) order to devote more time to his divine purpose.

He then moved to the holy city of Vrindavana where he became involved in years of deep study and writing. On September 17, 1959, he received sannyasa (renounced order of life) and was given the name A.C. Bhaktivedanta Swami, and settled down in the beautiful temple of Sri Sri Radha Damodar ji. The same year, he began working on what would become his masterpiece: a multivolume translation and commentary on the 18,000-verse Srimad-Bhagavatam (Bhagavata Purana). The next six years of his life were spent in intense Krishna bhakti. He took darshan of the famous deities of Madan Mohan ji, Govind ji, Gopinath ji, and Radha Raman ji regularly and performed intensive Krishna bhajan.

Venturing to the West Alone

Devotees of Lord Krishna firmly believe that anyone who dies in Vrindavan is guaranteed a place in Goloka, the eternal residence of Lord Krishna in the spiritual world. Many people therefore settle down in Vrindavan in their old age to achieve that eternal residence. Srila Prabhupada, however, was driven by the instruction he had received from his spiritual master in 1922 to go to the western world and preach Krishna Consciousness in English. So, in 1969, at the ripe old age of 69, he left the devotional world of Vrindavan and came to the USA in a cargo ship with merely 40 rupees and a trunk full of Srimad Bhagavatam books he had translated into English and written commentaries for. It was a difficult journey for an old man, and he suffered two heart attacks on the way. But his faith in Lord Krishna saved him and he landed in Boston on September 17, 1965. In Boston he wrote a heart wrenching poem expressing his surrender to Lord Krishna. An excerpt of that poem is given below.

Somehow or other, You have brought me here to speak about You. Now it is up to You to make me a success or failure, as You like.

You are the Lord of the whole creation, so if You like You can make my power to speak suitable, so that they can understand.

By Your causeless mercy only my words may become transcendentally pure, and I am sure that when such a transcendental message penetrates their hearts, certainly they will feel engladdened and thus become liberated from all unhappy conditions of life.

I am just like a puppet in Your hands; You have brought me here, and now You can make me dance as You like.

Two days later the same ship took him to New York City from where he went to Butler, Pennsylvania to the house of an Indian gentleman and his American wife, who had sponsored him to come to America. The hosts ate meat every day and the wife smoked cigarettes. Srila Prabhupada simply told them, "Think nothing of it," and continued to focus on finding opportunities to share Krishna Consciousness. After two months, he returned to New York City, and continued his efforts there.

Struggling Alone

In New York, Srila Prabhupada or "swami ji", as he was then known, did not know anyone nor did he have a place of his own to stay. He ended up staying with another Swami, named Dr. Misra who preached a philosophy directly opposed to Gaudiya Vaishnava philosophy. Although Dr. Misra was kind to him and provided decent accommodation, it was painful for Bhaktivedanta Swami to listen to the "nonsense and offensive" philosophy day after day. But he tolerated and was grateful for the hospitality. In the meantime, he would cook nice prasadam (sanctified vegetarian food offered to Lord Krishna and remnants accepted as Lord's mercy) for Dr. Misra and his disciples. Dr. Misra did allow Swami ji to chant the Hare Krishna Mahamantra "Hare Krishna Hare Krishna Krishna Krishna Hare Hare/ Hare Rama Hare Rama Rama Rama Hare Hare" in his programs. The attendees really enjoyed the chanting and would often dance. In private, Dr. Misra and Srila Prabhupada would have a number of heated discussions on philosophy but Dr. Misra did not allow Srila Prabhupada to speak in public, except on rare occasions.

Once, while he sat alone in his apartment, the lights in his room suddenly went out. This was the famous New York City blackout on November 9, 1965 that lasted from 6 PM till 7 AM the next morning. It left the entire city without electricity, trapped 800,000 people in the city's subways, and affected more than thirty million people in nine states and three Canadian provinces. But Srila Prabhupada remained undisturbed and began chanting the Hare Krishna mantra on his beads. He knew that Lord Krishna would protect and guide him in all situations and he could keep his full attention on the utterance of the holy name of Lord Krishna.

Srila Prabhupada felt that the American people were receptive to India's culture, art and music, as well as its spirituality. Many Indian "gurus" had established themselves in America by teaching various forms of yoga including Transcendental Meditation and impersonalist philosophy. People like Ravi Shankar had become famous for their music. He noted that Christian missions were preaching all over the world and felt confident that devotees of Krishna could do the same by teaching the philosophy of Srimad Bhagavatam with a scientific approach. He felt that people were ready to hear and understand the messages of Srimad Bhagavatam, if preached through music and dance. He realized that to attract more people, he needed a building. But he had no funds. As it is, he was surviving on the kind donation of various people for his rent and food money. Concerned about his visitor's visa about to expire, he wrote to his god-brothers, some industrialists and other people he knew in India, asking for financial help, but did not receive any.

But he was not prepared to give up. He lived with all the inconveniences of New York City. Although opulent, the city suffered from many things that he found difficult to tolerate. For example, the sirens of fire engines and police cars, someone being attacked on the street below his apartment and crying out for help, the smell of dog stool, and drunken people lying around on the street; this was not easy to tolerate for an old sannyasi. He felt disturbed by all the news about the increasing number of young people dying from LSD and all the protests against America's participation in the Vietnam War. He was in below zero temperatures that he had never experienced in India, and he continued to roam around the city of New York in his dhoti and a coat given to him by Dr. Misra, not worried about slipping and falling on icy roads. Established yogis and other acquaintances tried to persuade him to take up the western ways such as wearing a suit, eating with knife and fork and becoming non-vegetarian. But he was not in America to learn their ways or gain technical knowledge. He said "I am not a beggar. I am a giver." So rather than take to the uncivilized "mlechha" ways of Americans, he wanted to teach them how to do things according to Vedic literature.

He continued to dream about one day traveling around the world with his sankirtan party (a group of devotees chanting and singing in accompaniment of various musical instruments, mainly mridanga and kartal) sharing the Krishna Consciousness philosophy in all major cities. He imagined the big buildings in the city being used for spreading Krishna Consciousness. Once he told someone that he could see temples full of devotees. He said, "I am not a poor man. I am rich. There are temples and books. They are existing, they are there, but time is separating us from them." He felt compassion for people who despite owning lots of property and being rich, felt empty inside due to lack of Krishna Consciousness and an excess of material attachments and desires. He tried to make some money by selling his books that he had brought from India.

A Glimmer of Hope

Finally, his efforts showed results and he was able to rent a storefront on 26 Second Avenue on the lower east side of New York City with the help of the young men who were now coming to hear him regularly. He made it his preaching centre and started to attract small crowds to his classes and kirtans. Ironically the store was named "Matchless Gifts" even before he started renting it.

He started going to the nearby Tompkins Square Park and chanted under a tree. He  attracted *Srila Prabhupada preaching at Tompkins Square Park* many young American hippies who joined in his chanting. Soon they started bringing their own instruments and joined him in Sankirtan (congregational chanting of Hare Krishna Mahamantra). Srila Prabhupada started to share Krishna Consciousness with these young people, some of whom actually became regular attendees and started to show serious interest in Krishna Consciousness and were willing to give up their materialistic, promiscuous, and drug-filled life style.

In 1966, Srila Prabhupada incorporated his organization as the "**I**nternational **S**ociety for **K**rishna **Con**sciousness" or ISKCON, and registered it in the city of New York, and the rest is history. ISKCON, which is also known as the Hare Krishna movement, is one of the fastest-growing spiritual movements in the history of the world.

He was invited to San Francisco to a tumultuous welcome by his followers and he organized the first Lord Jagannath Rath Yatra in the West. It was attended by thousands of people. Rath Yatra is now celebrated in all corners of the world with thousands in attendance. Every major city in Canada now celebrates Rath Yatra including the Greater Toronto Area which has 3 Rath Yatras every year, with the largest one attracting more than 40,000 visitors. The Rath Yatra in Durban, South Africa attracts over 300,000 people for a three day celebration.

Srila Prabhupada at Rath Yatra in San Francisco in 1967

Spiritual Momentum

Srila Prabhupada was conscious of his age and the limited time he had to complete his mission of spreading the Holy Name of the Lord in every nook and corner of this world, as per the prophecy made by Lord Chaitanya. He also wanted to write, publish, and distribute English translations of Vedic scriptures. He was a prolific writer who translated and wrote commentary on more than 70 books, and authored several books over the last two decades of his life. He slept an average only two hours a day. His books are popular all over the world and have been translated into 75 different languages.

He based his teachings mainly on the Bhagavat Gita and Srimad Bhagavatam. He made ISKCON or the Hare Krishna movement, as it is more popularly known, a household name everywhere. Everyone in the world seems to have heard the phrase "Hare Krishna Hare Rama." His work on Bhagavat Gita known as "Bhagavat Gita – As It Is" and Srimad Bhagavatam are considered by Vedic scholars as the finest translation of Vaishnava literary works. ISKCON's publishing arm, The Bhaktivedanta Book Trust (BBT) has become the largest publisher of religious literature with more than half a billion books in more than 75 languages already sold. There are more than a million followers of this movement around the world and Bhagavat Gita is now taught in many schools and colleges around the world.

Srila Prabhupada traveled across the globe 14 times in 12 years establishing centres and farm communities, building or acquiring temples, and making thousands of devotees. He sent his disciples to Canada, Europe, behind the iron curtain in the former Soviet Union,

Africa, Australia and China. It did not matter that these disciples had no money and in many cases, they did not speak the local language. They all succeeded after some initial difficulties.

Srila Prabhupada's gift to the world has been to teach us the most beneficial, simple method by which we can realize our eternal loving relationship with Supreme Lord Sri Krishna. And that method is to chant the holy names of the Lord: Hare Krishna Hare Krishna Krishna Krishna Hare Hare / Hare Rama Hare Rama Rama Rama Hare Hare. He gave this Mahamantra to everyone without any regard to age, gender, nationality, ethnic background, marital, health or economic status.

He emphasized that Bhagavat Gita was not a religious book but a practical guide for human beings to live together happily and peacefully through understanding the following basic principles:

- *We are not this body, rather spirit soul. The purpose of our human life is to learn how to love God*
- *The supreme Lord Krishna is the controller of everything that happens, and is our well wisher. Our role in life is to serve the Lord and fully depend on him for all our needs*
- *The only way to get out of this material world which is full of struggles is to surrender to the Lord*

Millions around the world are reading and following the instructions of Bhagavat Gita and Srimad Bhagavatam and feeling the bliss. There are more than 650 temples, farm communities including goshalas (cow sheds), and centres in the world providing local residents the knowledge of the scriptures in their native languages, and engaging them in the service to the Lord. Thousands of devotees around the world are regularly inviting their neighbours to their homes to tell them about Krishna Consciousness, encourage them to read books written by Srila Prabhupada, answer questions, remove doubts and make friends. Millions are also visiting holy places such as Vrindavan and Mayapur due to the descriptions they have read in the books of Srila Prabhupada. The sight of devotees chanting and dancing in the streets of cities around the world is no longer considered unusual. The local residents and tourists with no knowledge of what it is happily join in. It is predicted that people will continue to benefits from these books for the next 10,000 years. It is all because of the tireless efforts of one old man who showed up in America with just 40 rupees in his pocket!! One man changed the lives of millions for the better.

The emergence & expansion of the problems of the people of Indian Origin

Rinkal Sharma[6]

The world is a family
One is a relative, the other stranger, say the small minded.
The entire world is a family, live the magnanimous.
—Maha Upanishad 6.71–7

"VasudhaivaKutumbakam" (वसुधैवकुटुम्बकम्) is a Sanskrit phrase written in Hindu Upanishad - the Maha Upanishad, which means "The world is one family". This phrase VasudhaivaKutumbakam consists of Three words: "Vasudhā" which means the earth, "ēva" means indeed, and "Kutumbakam" means family. People of India who cross their shores for different reasons, probably have this notion very firmly ingrained in their mind and heart. They are believer that The world is a family, and they would get positive and better life even outside their home shore as complete world is a family.

The Indian Diaspora encompasses a group of people who can either trace their origins to India or who are Indian citizens living abroad, either temporarily or permanently. These people are broadly classified by Indian government in 2 major category - People of Indian Origin (PIO), while a sub-set of this is the Non-resident Indian (NRI). Persons of Indian Origin (PIOs) and Overseas Citizens of India (OCI) card holders were merged under OCI category in 2015. Overseas Indiansare people of Indian birth, descent or origin who live outside the Republic of India. Overseas Indians are various individuals or ethnic groups associated with India, usually through ancestry,

---

[6] Rinkal Sharma, Delhi, India

ethnicity, nationality, citizenship or other affiliation and live abroad overseas.

According to a Ministry of External Affairs report, there were 30,995,729 NRIs and PIOs residing outside India as of December 2018. According to the United Nations Department of Economic and Social Affairs based on migrants overseas with India as the country of citizenship at birth, in 2019 Indians comprised world's largest migrant diaspora populations in the world with over 17.5 million (6.4% of global migrants or 0.4% of India's population) Indians out of total 272 million migrants worldwide, this excludes the second or more-generation POI living in other nations. As per last data published by India's ministry of overseas affairs, over 30 million people of Indian origin do not live in India. Indian Emigrants are usually defined as those overseas Indians who claim India to be their birthplace. They are usually referred to as non-resident Indians (NRIs), though some have also given up their citizenship after naturalization.

From 21st January to 23rd January, India celebrated its 15th Pravasi Bhartiya Diwas. Thanks to the efforts of former Prime Minister of India, Late Sh. Atal Bihari Vajpayee, India every year celebrates its **Pravasi Bhartiya Diwas** on 9th January to commemorate return of its most iconic and beloved Pravasi (Indian Emigrant) Mahatma Gandhi from Africa on 9th January 1915. However, migration from India started way back. Going into the past & looking when migration really started from Indian shores, a clue is available in book "Migrant Asia" written by RadhakamalMukerjee in 1936, as the basic premise of the book is that labour-surplus regions in Asia, especially India, should have the option of redistributing its population around the world. It would be welfare-improving for everybody. Historical records suggest that India's own brush with mass migration started in the century following 1834, as nearly 40 million people had moved overseas in, when organized recruitment for work in the plantations of Mauritius began during the colonial era.

Focussing in last 50 years, from the 1970s thanks to globalization, Indian emigration began to surge to a point where, by some estimates, there are more emigrants of Indian origin today than from any other country in the world. With the technology emergence in a rapid manner, easier mode of communication & travel, Indian migration numbers, better call large chunk of aspirational India youth, started rising & continuing even today to the extent that even politicians starting from Prime Minister Narendra Modi to former Congress president Rahul Gandhi make it a point to court overseas Indians in their most of the speeches in & outside India, making them an important consequential bloc of non-voters in the country.

The Indian Diaspora

Over the past 50-70 years largely, Indian emigration has made two fundamental but major switches. In context of mass movements within Asia, emigration from the country's eastern seashore toward South-East Asia has been replaced by emigration from the west coast toward the Persian Gulf countries, which now account for approximately half of India's emigrants. Burma's strict 1982 citizenship law, economic and regulatory shock across the Bay of Bengal are one of the main reasons behind this major shift. Also, to a large extent, unbelievable frenetic growth of oil-based economies across the Arabian Sea resulted economic growth and big-time employment opportunities which was another attraction behind Indian emigration.

Outside Asia, life was not found rosy to Indian emigration as African & South American countries fell out of radar favour as with the change of time & trade, the needs of the old plantation-based economies of the colonial empire changed. While on other hand, Europe and North America attained reputation as racist visa walls were torn down in the second half of the 20th century. Due to these changes in dynamics, different categories of overseas Indians based on their requirements, need, dreams & aspiration, have come into the limelight.

Getting citizenship in the host country is not the privilege extended in the Persian Gulf countries which absorb the bulk of NRIs, with the United Arab Emirates (UAE) emerging as the single largest destination with over three million Indians. As per current set of published data, Indian emigrants majorly covers for one third of UAE's total population. Also, PIOs make up a substantial part of the local population in Mauritius, Fiji, Trinidad and Tobago, Guyana, Suriname, Reunion Island, and to a much lesser extent in South Africa, Kenya and Uganda. Indian example of large-scale migration began during the British rule as indentured labourers to former colonies like Fiji, Kenya and Malaysia (also known as Girmitiya people).

Rinkal Sharma

In last 50 years, United States as global power, has emerged out as the most important diaspora destination not only for Indian emigrants but across globe as well, India itself has grown to become the second most important source of immigrants in the US, very close to US neighbour Mexico. This set of Indian emigration to the US has been and still is typically high-skilled in nature in Information & computer technology, medical and other emerging technology domain, along with student migration as the first step towards job employment. Needless to mention, this is the reason why Political scientist Devesh Kapur and others in a recent book have mentioned Indians in the US as the "other one per cent", referring to the share of Indians in the American population as well as the high-income nature of their occupations.

As per common conception, majority of Indian emigrants are from the states of Punjab, Gujarat and southern states of India. Punjab's historic affinity for all things Canada & UK is a known fact. Singapore, Australia, and New Zealand are other parts of the English-speaking world that have witnessed a surge in Indian emigration over the past decade.

In last 2 decades, Indian diaspora is more widely scattered than ever before and is drawn from several parts of India. This new diaspora is relatively more permanently settled in North America and Europe where it is also more gender-balanced and is less diverse in its caste composition than the old diaspora.

Focussing on expansion of the problems of the people of Indian Origin, a notion generally emerges out once you communicate with these Indian Emigrants, that many of them live with the thought of returning home every single day. Nonetheless, when it comes to actually doing it, the anxiety truly hits them. This dilemma is bigger for those who went abroad for higher studies and had never worked in India. The fear of giving it all up and diving into the deep unknown is, needless to mention, quite terrifying. The other thing which this fraternity hint mainly, As NRIs, abroad, life is not all rosy. There are problems there too. They get to work very hard and get to adjust to foreign cultures and so on. In the beginning, as it is new to them & they learn new things at a terrific pace, which keep them happy for a while. But once this learning levels off, and life begins to get mundane. They have to live with traffic problems (not just admiring smooth roads), housing problems (not just admire the neat and clean houses), too-much-housework problems (not just admire the great equipment), health-insurance problems (not just admire the great medical technology), and finally, just-too-mechanical-living problems. And on top of this, there are the bigger issues: do they still want to be here when they are retired? Will they end up totally alone in my old age? How the family, kids will be in connect with their culture back in India? How to manage if feel an emptiness in soul that is very difficult to get rid of. And so on.

India of course, has its own set of problems. I don't need to go into them in detail, because we all know what those problems are. Many times, it is very difficult to decide whether to go back home if they aren't fully happy in our host nation. How to deal & not to succumb to the mundaneness of everyday living. Either to live with the problems abroad, or to live with the problems in India, both options have problems associated with them.

Emigrants are not one big blob who have same problems. Even a typical problem may vary from person to person. There are millions of NRIs and they can have millions of "typical" problems, which will be difficult to write here. For example, a typical NRI living in the Europe will have problem with the language, whereas a typical NRI living in the USA will not have that same problem (hopefully). While on the other hand, a typical NRI living in USA may have a problem with healthcare, and that is not the case with a typical NRI living in the Europe. The thing with typical problems is that they can be quite typical, and if the problem is typical for one, it can be no problem at all for another. Problems are never same, they are as varied as the individual. And NRIs are individuals with very typical individual problems. However, for large chunk of emigrants faces similar kind of challenges & problems.

Challenges for Indian Emigrants Outside India

1. **Home sickness, emotionally dying feeling of staying away from family & friends who were with you since childhood**

Life without your loved ones, family & friends is difficult to live. This ubiquitous pain can be easily felt during conversation with NRIs. Video calls and sharing photos with parents and family back in India is not a substitution for maintaining real family relationships.

2. **Inability to be with your relatives and family in their good and bad times**

When Pankaj Udhas sang "ChitthiAyihai" in Movie - Naam, as much poignant as the song was, one could take solace in the fact that at least only the son is overseas while the rest of the family and support system could still be with the parents.It is thought provoking that when the world around us has seemed to shrink with several modes of communications at our disposal, still the bitter feeling of staying away from your parent, family, friends is indeed a killing feeling to have. Luckier are those who have someone to take care of family in India, as they are is there with ageing parents whenever they are in need. But such condition is difficult to handle by those who are no support at home to take care, or with single child. Feeling of such guilt kills the person within.

There is always more socialising in India and people are closed to each other- which makes a lot of difference in life.

3. **Rising incidence of hate speech and crimes against Indian Diaspora by the locals due to racism, communalism emboldened by coming of nationalist and ultra nationalist governments to power in many countries**

Such news, which has started coming out more frequently in recent past, are indeed very disturbing. Many times, people at native land or abroad, both wonder if these incidences will only increase in future, considering the patience fatigue attitude of Today's human who has almost crossed line of intolerance, inhumanity & self-centredness. Gaining political advantages by bashing foreigners in their country is the cheapest way to get publicity & political mileage. Such kind of politics & politicians don't survive in field for long, as soon people recognise that their hatred is not against outsiders, they have their own political motive behind all these.But sad part is, such incidences don't only harm the victim but to large set of people who are directly or indirectly associated with him. These incidenceshappen for no fault of victim, most of the times.

4. **Economy Slow-down/ Increasing anti-globalization: Fear of unemployment, losing jobs and educational opportunities to outsiders has resulted in stricter visa rules in many countries including USA, Australia etc.**

One thing NRIslearn very quickly is that abroad, life is not all rosy. There are problems there too. An unknowing but always available around threat of managing life in those difficult situations/period which almost everyone must go through in their life. In recent time due to rapid change in technologies, faced paced development, frequent cases of economy slow-down or attribute it to increasing anti-globalization, uncertainty in future is always like a monkey on your back which is getting weight with each success in life. Many times, carrying this regularly gaining weight monkey, is very difficult to carry for lifetime.

5. **Laws in favour of locals towards employment - Adverse local laws to encourage more employment from locals such as Nitaqat Law of Saudi Arabia (mandates one local to be hired in place of 10 migrants) has adversely affected prospects of the Indian working class in Saudi Arabia**

6. **Sectarian crisis, increasing racial &terrorist activities and war in the Middle East countries (Yemen, Oman, Libya, Syria etc) leave Indian diaspora vulnerable to attacks**

Citizens from other countries are soft target of notorious citizens, criminals, racist, terrorists or religious extremist, as loss to them hurt not only to host nation but to the nation where he victim belongs to. They are more vulnerable to be attacked. There are so many instances in recent past.

7. **Feeling of outsiders & difficulty in adjusting with foreign culture**

Most of NRIs generally shares their pain of not able to fully adapt and get settled in the culture of host country, which leaves them with a sore feeling of outsiders. This painful feeling remain for lifelong.

8. **Excessive academic expectations**

Essentially, the crux of the issue confronting all NRIs is the weight of expectation one thrusts on the younger generation and the illusion with which they subject themselves oblivious of the practical consequences of the choices that they have made in their lives.There is a good side also, but the trade-offs are different for every individual.

Whether it is getting into Harvard or being the top in the school, there is no dearth of obsessive competition. The poor second-generation kid is subject to immense pressure and his/her talents is confined to the narrow path of engineering and no other streams of study. Not only does this reduce the appetite for the children, it makes their options and mindset for the future narrow. It is more of the NRI parent imposing what "they" want to be rather than what the "children" want to be. The main issue is the massive expectation they have from their children and therein lies the crux of the next issue confronting the NRIs.

9. **Many people are lonely because in the end, it is not easy to make friends and even they are able to have a social circle, everyone is busy in their lives. Even the office environment is different- people don't interact much- because of hourly pay, they finish their work and go home. Only time to interact is Friday evenings or in get-together events/Party**

Stuck in the vicious cycle of money and social pressures, they are not able to break away from the social barriers to return home.

10. Ignorance

Many a times, People from India Origin have to deal with ignorance of host country citizens toward them, as on saying I am Indian receives the response, "what tribe?" People do not know that Hindu is not an ethnicity, that Hindi is not a religion, and that Indian is not a language. They also, for the most part, assume Hinduism is a polytheistic ancient religion, similar to the Greeks and Romans.

11. Identity Crisis

This is the biggest one. Next generation of NRIs in most cases grew up believing they needed blonde hair and blue eyes to be beautiful, that speaking a language other than English was weird, and that showing up in public with Indian clothes was embarrassing. It takes a long time for them to accept their heritage as something special, and they are still not fully there today.

12. **Though not common, but somewhere people are always scared about being deported- until they gain citizenship/residency, which is why people who go abroad only think about getting residency first**

13. **Managing everything on your own& to manage high cost of living- rent, insurance, health (if not subsidized), maintenance of car and home- as labour is not cheap at all**

Summarizing for large chunk of Indian emigrants, Most NRIs get trapped into the vicious circle of corporate jobs, so deeply that the professional priorities overtake family relationships. Most NRIs get trapped into the immigration issues so deeply that life will become a series of sacrifices.

Challenges for Indian Emigrants in India

1. Brain-Drain impacting speed of growth of India – Rising number of Indian emigration results in substantial drop in the supply of skilled and competent professionals for running institutions and organisations in India.

2. NRIs are largely seen as source of foreign money in-flow, which help Indian Government in welfare schemes. Pity is remittances are not always used for beneficial purposes. Many times in recent past, there have been cases of foreign funding used for activities against nation. For instance, India faced problems due to foreign funding for extremist movements like the Khalistan movement.

3. The NRIs are not allowed to set up their firms directly in India due to which India is not able to take full advantage of their entrepreneurial skills.

4. E-Migrate system and the Minimum Referral Wages policy have been detrimental to India as companies now find it easier to hire labour from countries like Bangladesh and Pakistan.

5. Poor schemes coupled with ineffectual implementation hinder the Diasporas' contribution towards the growth of India

Timely and a solid investment for future needs is one of the most sought-after goal among Indians and NRIs both. For NRIs though it becomes a more confusing process since they do not reside here. The struggle is real in real estate.

6. Finding the right kind of investment in property is always a struggle, especially by Non-resident Indians (NRIs) as they often face several issues while they plan to invest in Indian real estate market.

7. Lack of clarity & confusion over taxations &legal rights

When investing in real estate, there is a lack of clarity on the legal rights of NRI investors when they invest in India. The locals sometimes dupe them by selling illegal lands thereby leading to huge losses for them. Moreover, since NRIs stay overseas, it gets difficult for them to be updated with the latest news and reforms in the Indian real estate.

NRIs also suffer because they unknowingly invested in the wrong project or the work got delayed by the developers. Punjab and Haryana which have the largest population of NRIs have reported the highest fraud cases as the local dupe buyers by selling farmland and agricultural land illegally. Many NRI investors have suffered because of their investment in the wrong project and real estate developer who have delayed their projects.

8. Delay in process

A lot of NRIs complain that when it comes to investment, there are a lot of background checks that lead to delay in services and time loss. Most of them face issues when they have to invest money in their NRE, NRO or FCNR accounts. That's why NRIs need to use the banking services of a place that has a smooth process and have credibility in the market.

More than half of the issues arise for NRIs because of their advisors who are dubious and know how to take advantage of them. It's very important to have a trustworthy source of advice.

9. Financial Discrimination

The tax rules for NRIs are quite different from those that apply to normal residents. There is no tax on foreign income but still, the tax reporting is quite elaborate, the TDS rules are stiff and NRIs don't enjoy some of the tax privileges that resident citizens enjoy. There is a long list of rules that one needs to know before going in for any kind of investment whether big or small. Once you know all the rules, then it's suitable to think what kind and how much of an investment you are ready to make. A few steps taken in the right direction can secure future and help reap benefits of investment sooner and hassle-free in a foreign shore.

10. Land grabbing issues

Illegal possession, gatecrashing is another challenge faced by NRIs if they are investing in India. In fact, in majority of the cases, the land grabber and person taking illegal possession is known to the buyer.

Solution framework to handle NRI's challenges

1. To stop brain-drain and to use expertise of NRIs to create skilled & competent professionals, India should formalise a rotation program wherein top NRI scientists, engineers, doctors, managers and professionals serve Indian public sector organizations for a brief period, lending their expertise, like VAJRA Scheme.

2. In last 15-20 years, Indian government is aggressively courting NRIs to invest in India. Attracting NRIs to invest in India has always been top priority of all the central & state governments during the tenure. This is win-win situation for all the stakeholders.

3. India should open a separate Minister-of-State level department for NRI administration - like the Veterans' Administration in the US.

4. Social media tools have made it easy and inexpensive for Indian Diaspora to stay in touch with family and friends back home, and their link to India has never been stronger. It is time that the Indian government leveraged this strong bond for the greater good of the nation.One of the greatest benefits of engaging with the 30-million-strong Indian diaspora has been in terms of remittances.

The Indian Diaspora – Very important role to play for India's Growth

1. As per data available, Remittances close to 69 billion dollar make an invaluable contribution by aiding Government in various welfare schemes in socio-economic development, Infrastructure development etc.

2. Another mode of contribution by NRIs is to NGOs or Charitable trusts, as they are more prone to donating to domestic charities because of the strong cultural and feelings that they nurse over a period of years. A feeling of returning something to the country is always in their heart. And trust, this is the most pleasant feeling to have and to respect and appreciate.

3. Another tangible long-term advantage in nurturing ties with an active Diaspora is an accelerated technological sector. Since technology is rapidly changing, NRIs and their experience can be highly beneficial in the growth of sector.

4. Diaspora acts as 'agents of change' facilitating and enhancing investment, accelerating industrial development, and boosting international trade and tourism.

5. Migration of skilled labours to foreign countries and their eventual success bolstered the nation's image.

6. The migration of less-skilled labour (especially to West Asia) has also helped in bringing down disguised unemployment in India.

7. A less tangible but important advantage in having a large emigrant group is "diaspora diplomacy" and they act as "bridge-builders" between their home and

adopted countries. Indo-US Civil Nuclear Deal is a case in point, as ethnic Indians in United States successfully lobbied for clinching of the N-deal.

8. Diaspora's motives to invest in India are in contrast to non-diaspora FDI. Their investments are long lasting as many of them wish to establish a long-term base in India.

Indian Government Initiative towards "Rashtradoots" - Their own people "NRIs"

1. In words of Indian prime minister, Indian diaspora are our 'Rashtradoots'. He addressed Indian diaspora in different parts of the world from Madison Square, New York to Kigali, Rawanda. Indeed, NRIs are pride of India.

2. Government's initiatives towards the diaspora are two-pronged. Firstly, non-residents are provided with consular services, protection and outreach activities.

3. At the same time, policies are created to encourage the diaspora to contribute in India's growth through philanthropy, knowledge transfers, and investments in development projects.

4. There is a Memorandum of Understanding (MOU) between the Ministry of External Affairs (MEA) and the Ministry of Skill Development and Entrepreneurship (MSDE) for implementation of the Pravasi Kaushal Vikas Yojana (PKVY), with objective of the Scheme is to institutionalize the process of skill development of emigrant Indian workers, provide them basic knowledge about laws, language and culture of the destination countries for the purpose of overseas employment.

5. The Scheme also aims at capacity building in the country in the area of development of standards, learning material, assessment standards, testing and certification on par with global standards.

6. Indian Government has also launched Scholarship Programme for Diaspora Children (SPDC) under which 100 scholarships per annum are granted to Persons of Indian Origin (PIO) and Non Resident Indians (NRI) students for undergraduate courses.

7. Know India Program' (KIP) is a flagship initiative for Diaspora engagement which familiarizes Indian-origin youth (18-30 years) with their Indian roots and contemporary India.

8. Under Minimum Referral Wages (MRW), applicable to Emigration Check Required (ECR) countries, India has increased the minimum wages of Indian workers employed as industrial workers, domestic servants, cleaners and labourers.

9. E-migrate system requires all foreign employers to register in the database. It ensures the welfare and check on exploitation met to emigrants.

10. Indian government has also started Madad Portal to take timely and speedy action on grievances addressed by people living abroad.

11. The Government of India has given several incentives to NRIs for investing their funds in India. They are exempt from several taxes and other charges. NRI seats are reserved in all the medical, engineering and other professional colleges.

The Representation of the People (Amendment) Bill 2017 the provision would help non-resident Indians (NRIs) to participate in the electoral process. It extends the facility of 'proxy voting' to overseas Indians, on the lines of service voters.

www.ingramcontent.com/pod-product-compliance
Lightning Source LLC
Chambersburg PA
CBHW081352080526
44588CB00016B/2469